CW00957664

FEAR AND GREED

INVESTMENT RISKS AND OPPORTUNITIES IN A TURBULENT WORLD

NICOLAS SARKIS

HARRIMAN HOUSE LTD
3A Penns Road
Petersfield
Hampshire
GU32 2EW
GREAT BRITAIN

Tel: +44 (0)1730 233870
Fax: +44 (0)1730 233880
Email: enquiries@harriman-house.com
Website: www.harriman-house.com

First edition published in 2012.

This edition published in 2012. Copyright © Harriman House Ltd

The right of Nicolas Sarkis to be identified as the author has been asserted in accordance with the Copyright, Design and Patents Act 1988.

978-0-85719-243-1

British Library Cataloguing in Publication Data
A CIP catalogue record for this book can be obtained from the British Library.

Printed and bound by CPI Group (UK) Ltd, Croydon, CR0 4YY.

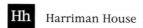 Harriman House

To Bob
My mentor at Goldman Sachs – a great figure I have always admired,
who later became Under Secretary of the United States Treasury under
Hank Paulson's leadership

To Bulat
The most exceptional and talented businessman I have ever met – a
truly inspirational figure

Contents

About the Author   VII

Acknowledgements   IX

Introduction   XI

1.   A Lost Era in Equities   1

2.   Will Deleveraging Drag us Down?   21

3.   Gold's Glittering Path   41

4.   Beyond hype: a Balanced Look at Emerging Markets   63

5.   Dread, Denial and Default   87

6.   The Future of the Euro   107

7.   Fear and Loathing on Wall Street   127

8.   When Rules and Regulators Fail   149

9.   The Moral Hazard of Money   169

10.   Central Banks: Leave, Improve or Abolish?   189

Conclusion   217

Index   219

ABOUT THE AUTHOR

NICOLAS SARKIS started his career in 1993 as an Associate with Goldman Sachs' Institutional Equities division in New York. He relocated to London in 1994. He became a Vice President in 1997, at the age of 26. He spent more than 12 years with Goldman Sachs where he was successively Head of the US Shares institutional sales and trading group in Europe and then a Vice President in the Private Wealth Management (PWM) department where he worked for about 9 years.

While in the US Shares group, Sarkis and his team ranked number one in the McLagan Survey of Institutional Investors three years in a row, providing equity research coverage to several of the largest European institutional investors and successfully placing many high profile Initial Public Offerings of the 1990s – Ralph Lauren, Steinway Pianos, Associates First Capital, Real Network, China Telecom – as well as secondary block trades – e.g. the sale of BP stake by the Kuwait Investment Office.

While in PWM, Sarkis managed investment portfolios for some of Europe's wealthiest families and largest foundations. When he left Goldman Sachs at the end of 2005, Sarkis was running one of Goldman's largest PWM teams in Europe.

Sarkis set up AlphaOne Partners at the beginning of 2006 as he felt he could put together a more pertinent service offering for very large investors from the vantage point of a buy-side institutional investment platform. Such investors are typically those whose assets are too large to be managed by a bank.

AlphaOne's model revolves around three simple principles:

i)   conflict-of-interest free investment advice – AlphaOne does not have any in-house products and investors are not shareholders

ii)   improved investment methodology by focusing on a tried and tested investment process, similar to that used by the most successful university endowments globally

iii)   cutting transaction and management fees whenever possible, thanks to AlphaOne's institutional investor status

IN MAY 2008, the *Wall Street Journal Europe* ranked AlphaOne amongst Europe's top wealth advisers; it was the only firm in the top 5 of this annual ranking which was not affiliated with a banking institution. In January 2009, AlphaOne ranked at the top of Wall Street Journal's Wealth Bulletin investment management league table. In December 20009, *Spears*, one of the UK's leading wealth management magazines, chose AlphaOne to be the recipient of its annual asset management award.

ACKNOWLEDGEMENTS

In the course of writing this book, I have been fortunate enough to have had access to some of the finest economic and financial databases in existence. These collections of market data are the result of many years of painstaking research by their creators. I want to express my gratitude to them all publicly for their generosity in making their invaluable findings available to me.

In no particular order, I would like to thank Professor Carmen M. Reinhart of the Peterson Institute for International Economics for her permission to cite figures from the database of government indebtedness that she assembled with Professor Kenneth S. Rogoff of Harvard University.

Likewise, I am thankful to Professor Robert S. Shiller of Yale University for letting me quote from his figures relating to US stock returns, inflation and interest rates going back to 1871.

My task was also made considerably easier by perusing the superb compendium of global asset price performance compiled by Professor Elroy Dimson of London Business School, and his colleagues Paul Marsh and Mike Staunton, and which is published annually as the *Credit Suisse Global Investment Returns Yearbook* and *Sourcebook*.

My thanks also go to Professor David Le Bris of Université Paris-Sorbonne, France, for supplying me with the superb recreation of France's CAC 40 index going back to 1854 that he constructed with Professor Pierre-Cyrille Hautcoeur of the Paris School of Economics.

I am also indebted to Chris Chantrill for letting me include figures derived from his website (**www.ukpublicspending.co.uk**).

INTRODUCTION

THE GLOBAL FINANCIAL CRISIS that erupted in 2007 has dramatically transformed the world of investment. Many trillions of dollars of wealth have been destroyed, with few types of financial asset immune from the carnage. The ultimate owners of much of this lost wealth – the general public – now hold the investment industry in lower esteem than they ever have before, and understandably so. A great deal of what we investors thought we knew about markets and investment also lies in tatters.

I have witnessed the markets' extreme fear and greed of recent years in about the most direct way possible. Throughout the period, I have worked as an investment manager, advising both individuals and institutions what to do with billions of dollars of their funds. Having worked for Goldman Sachs for a dozen years, I established my own investment firm – AlphaOne Partners – in early 2006, a mere eighteen months before the crisis struck. To say that this business underwent a baptism of fire is clearly an understatement.

It is one of my proudest achievements that I have helped AlphaOne's investors not only to protect but also to grow their wealth amidst these torrid conditions. Without wishing to sound immodest, I believe that we have been able to do this because we had well-formed ideas about the sort of opportunities that the crisis was likely to create and were thus well prepared for them when they arose. These included successful investments in stocks, commodities, real estate and private equity. Being prepared is essential, as the window of opportunity in these instances is often brief.

It was in the spirit of preparing for the next set of opportunities that I decided to write this book. As of late spring 2012, the financial crisis is still very much with us. Harsh but necessary austerity measures are biting savagely across much of Europe, casting people out of work and crimping living standards. There is a genuine risk that the single European currency will not survive in its current form, and that some developed world countries will end up defaulting on their debts. Investors need to have a plan in the event of one or both of these disastrous scenarios.

Even if the euro survives and if sovereign defaults are avoided, however, the coming years will still present enormous challenges to investors. Reducing indebtedness across the developed world is set to affect economic growth and investment returns for a long time to come. Deleveraging – as this process is known – poses an especially serious risk to those who hold government bonds, but also to anyone with ordinary savings. The freedom of investment choice that we have gained over recent decades could come under threat.

While one purpose of this book is to provide inspiration about how to invest in the years ahead, its lessons are drawn largely from history, and not just from that of the recent past. The difficulties for stock markets in the West began not with the credit crunch in 2007, but at the turn of the millennium. I argue that the period since then is merely the latest in a series of lost eras for equities that have occurred regularly over the last two centuries. During these lost eras, equities can easily struggle for a decade and half, until they become genuinely cheap once more. I believe we may still be some way from reaching that point.

As well as asking when today's lost era for developed-market equities is likely to end, I have considered the outlook for two of the best-performing asset classes of recent years. Emerging-market equities and gold have delivered stellar returns since the start of the

21st century. Both have now acquired an enthusiastic following, which is something that experience suggests should make us cautious. Nevertheless, I believe that these asset classes could yet have a crucial role going forward.

It is not just wealth that requires rebuilding in the years ahead. Trust in the financial industry has also been destroyed on a grand scale. This may well prove much harder to repair than lost capital. The investing public has endured a steady succession of cases of outright fraud and financial wrongdoing, to whose perpetrators I have devoted a chapter. However, the public has also been badly let down by those who were supposed to protect them, namely central banks and financial regulators. I ask some fundamental questions here about their future roles.

The chapters in this book therefore fall into two categories. The first six chapters are mostly to do with the outlook for specific investments and market themes: equities (chapter 1), deleveraging (chapter 2), gold (chapter 3), emerging markets (chapter 4), government defaults (chapter 5) and the euro (chapter 6). The last four chapters address some bigger picture issues: fearfulness among investors (chapter 7), regulation (chapter 8), fraudsters and their victims (chapter 9), and the future of central banking (chapter 10). While I have grouped them in this way, the chapters can be read either sequentially or as standalone pieces.

Nicolas Sarkis
London, July 2012

Chapter 1

A Lost Era in Equities

Following a century to remember, the stock market has suffered more than a period – of longer than a decade – that many investors would rather forget. Equities were the best performing asset class across much of the globe between 1900 and 2000, despite some spectacular upsets along the way. Since the dawn of the new millennium, however, shares in the developed world have delivered decidedly disappointing returns, inferior to those on most of the main rival asset classes.

A holding of worldwide shares worth $1 at the start of the 20th century would have grown to be worth $7,632 by the end of it. By comparison, $1 in worldwide bonds would have turned into just $75, while $1 of cash invested safely would have become only $54. The tables have since turned dramatically, however. In the first decade of the 21st century, a $1 investment in stocks would have grown to just $1.09 by 2010, versus $2.16 for bonds and $1.31 for cash.[1] Equities have significantly underperformed other assets.

Despite stocks' dismal showing since the dawn of the new millennium, the *cult of equity* remains largely intact. The cornerstone of this faith is that shares are the best bet when it comes to investing over extended periods of time. Its scriptures come in the form of such compelling research as that of Professor Jeremy Siegel, whose bestselling book *Stocks for the Long Run* has even been praised as "the buy-and-hold bible."[2] Unsurprisingly, one of this cult's most popular messages today is that, after such a lousy run since 2000, the stock market ought soon to resurrect itself.

Rather than obediently joining the flock, there is a strong case for questioning the orthodoxy on equities. While common stocks have indeed been winners over the very long run, there have also been times when they have struggled for a sustained period. Even in the US – the best performing market of all and the one for which the most detailed data exists – there have now been four periods from the early 20th century to the present when stocks have peaked, declined and then taken a generation or more to recover their former heights. I call these periods *lost eras*.

Fairly little has been said about these lost eras in equities compared to other episodes within stock-market history. After all, spectacular bubbles like the late 1990s tech mania and awesome crashes like that of October 1987 make for much racier reading. As a result, ordinary investors are largely in the dark about the very existence of these lost eras, let alone about their characteristics or what caused them. For obvious reasons, the cult of equity's high priests – the banks and brokerage houses that dominate the financial industry today – prefer not to dwell excessively on these inconvenient, but very significant, exceptions.

While less sophisticated players may well prefer to kneel and pray that the poor returns on stocks since 2000 will soon somehow be miraculously transformed into a new bull market, serious investors should instead delve into the history books. By understanding what happened during previous periods of equity famine, we will be better prepared to cope with the challenges of the latest one – and position our portfolios accordingly.

So, let's begin by asking ourselves what exactly is a lost era in the stock market?

DEFINING A LOST ERA

LOOKING AT A CHART of the price-to-earnings ratio (PE) of US equities adjusted for inflation over the past 140 years or so (Chart 1.1), these periods are easy enough to spot. Whereas the long-term tendency has evidently been for stocks to rise, there are also clearly some long stretches of time where the market has gone downwards or sideways in a persistent fashion. The beginning of each lost era is the point where the stock market makes a major high that is subsequently not surpassed for many years.

CHART 1.1 – S&P 500 PRICE-TO-EARNINGS (PE) RATIO AFTER INFLATION, 1881 TO 2012

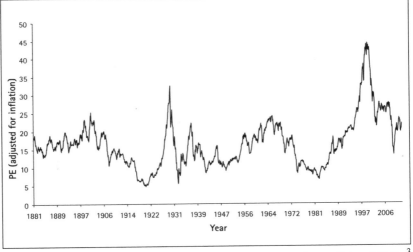

Source: Robert J. Shiller[3]

The timing of the end of a lost era isn't always quite as obvious as one might think, though. For two out of the three previous lost eras shown in Chart 1 – those that ended in 1920 and 1982 – the stock market's absolute low also marked the start of the next long-term uptrend. Following the Wall Street Crash of 1929, however, stocks hit rock-bottom in 1932 but the market essentially then went sideways – albeit with some dramatic swings in each direction – until the next sustained uptrend finally got underway in 1949, some 17

3

years later. And it wasn't for another decade still, until 1959, that the S&P finally regained its peak of 30 years earlier.

Measured from each stock-market peak to the time of the beginning of the next major uptrend, America's three lost eras of the 20th century lasted some 14, 20 and 14 years respectively. From the peak of the previous uptrend to the absolute lows, the S&P 500 shed more than 60 per cent of its value after inflation in each of these three periods. Looking back even further to America's two episodes of the early 19th century, stocks lost half and three-quarters of their real value. Interestingly, the three episodes in the 20th century were noticeably longer than the two lost eras of the 19th century, when the losses suffered were of a similarly major degree, but which nonetheless came to an end after seven years each time. We shall consider a possible reason for this later on. Of course, it is not all one-way traffic during a lost era. Stocks can rally mightily in these periods. Following the horrendous meltdown on Wall Street of 1929-32, to give just one example, the S&P soared by 132 per cent between 1935 and 1937. It then subsequently gave up more than 60 per cent of its value over the next five years. In Japan, where the Nikkei 225 stock index peaked in 1989 and remains depressed more than 20 years later, there have also been five occasions during that period where stocks have gained more than 50 per cent, only then to resume their long-term downtrend. These episodes merely serve to lure investors back into equities but end up leaving them disappointed – not to mention poorer – before very long.

Whereas lost eras have been the exception rather than the rule for the US, they have been far more ubiquitous in many other countries. French equities were trapped in a secular downtrend for more than half of the period between 1854 and 2000.[4] Adjusting for inflation, French stocks also declined in five decades of the 20th century. By way of comparison, British stocks declined in only two decades of the same period.[5]

Why lost eras occur

While awareness of the existence of lost eras is crucial for investors, it is only the first step. A much bigger challenge is explaining why these periods of equity famine actually occur in the first place. Today's lost era in the West began in 2000, with the bursting of the technology bubble. One possibility, therefore, is that previous lost eras were also at least partly the result of bubbles having burst.

Bubbles

The mania for technology, media and telecom stocks that began in the late 1990s was a clear example of a bubble even before it burst – at least to the more far-sighted among investors. The NASDAQ 100 index – home to many firms from the hot industries of the day – soared by an incredible 1,092 per cent from the start of 1995 to its peak five years later. Such perpendicular gains are themselves often a warning sign that things are getting out of control.

Of course, spectacular stock-price increases can sometimes be justified – particularly if corporate earnings are growing at a similar pace or are projected to do so with good reason. But it is hard to argue that this was the case for the late 1990s. Not only did the US stock market as a whole reach its most extreme ever level of valuation in terms of earnings, but many of the favourite hi-tech companies of the day did not have any earnings – or even revenues, in certain cases.

To justify this orgy of speculation, enthusiasts claimed that the game had fundamentally changed. New technologies – such as the internet – were supposedly going to improve the economy's potential to grow forever. Turning received wisdom on its head, equities were even argued to be *less* risky than government bonds, rather than more so. And conventional cash-flow based techniques were abandoned and even ridiculed as being outmoded.

Aside from the vertical increases in stock prices and the fanciful arguments that the old rules no longer applied, other prominent bubble characteristics were clearly in evidence in the late 1990s. Edward Chancellor – a leading authority on financial-market manias – has listed other generic features of a bubble, including rampant credit growth, corruption and blind faith in the authorities' ability to prevent a sticky ending.[6] These traits were clearly evident in the 1990s tech bubble.

The other great lost era for equities of the present age also began with the implosion of a spectacular bubble. Japan's Nikkei 225 index shot up by 469 per cent between the summer of 1982 and the end of 1989. This boom too was fuelled by a cocktail of inappropriately low interest rates, generous – and often irresponsible – lending by banks, and a widespread sense of confidence in the superiority of the Japanese ways of business and finance.

All of these elements were also present in spades during the decade known as the roaring 1920s. Easy credit stoked debt-fuelled speculation in Florida real estate, while Wall Street got carried away with such exciting modern technologies as mass-market versions of radio and the motor car. Excessive confidence in the investment outlook was best encapsulated by the contemporary economist Irving Fisher, who infamously remarked that "stocks have reached what looks like a permanently high plateau." The Great Crash of 1929 got underway just three days later, wiping out much of the professor's own fortune.

A big problem with the theory that lost eras result from bubbles bursting is that the 20th century's other two lost eras in the US were not preceded by manias of the same sort. The 1960s did see something of a boom in the stocks of certain growth companies, in particular, as well as the initial proliferation of mutual funds. But the US stock market as a whole did not experience runaway price growth.

The S&P 500 index went up 84 per cent from the start of the decade to its peak in 1968. And while there was a big influx of novice investors into equities thanks to the arrival of mutual funds, the enthusiasm never came close to that of the late 1990s, where newcomers were so enthusiastic yet uninformed that they sometimes bought into a particular stock mistakenly, merely because its name or ticker was similar to that of a technology stock.

Likewise, even though there was certainly some evidence of exuberance in the stock market around the very start of the 20th century – when stocks rose 163 per cent between August 1896 and September 1906[7] – this hardly compares to the NASDAQ's meteoric ascent in the late 1990s, or to the six-fold increase in the US market during the roaring 1920s. The market finally came decisively unstuck when it emerged that the chairman of a leading financial institution of the day had been using the firm's assets in an attempt to manipulate the copper market.

So, bubbles are significant in that they preceded many lost eras of the past, but they cannot be the sole explanation for why these eras occur.

OVERVALUATION

While bubbles may not have preceded all of Wall Street's main lost eras, overvaluation certainly has done. Stocks obviously looked very expensive as the market was peaking both in 1929 and 2000. But they were also noticeably dear in the early 1900s and the late 1960s. This is pretty much true whichever valuation technique is used, whether comparing stock prices to earnings, dividends or company assets. When equity valuations get extremely high, they tend eventually to return to their long-term average. As they do so, they very often overshoot the average to the downside.

A popular way of measuring the valuation of stocks over history is to use the cyclically-adjusted price-to-earnings ratio (PE), an approach popularised by Professor Robert Shiller. Rather than comparing the stock market's current price with its most recent year's earnings, which is the standard approach, Professor Shiller's technique compares the market to its average earnings over the last ten years. The logic of this method is that it smoothes out a lot of the most distorting effects of the economic cycle, thereby giving us a more stable view.

Since 1881, America's S&P 500 index has on average traded on a multiple of 16 times its earnings of the previous decade. In advance of every lost era, however, this multiple has reached at least 24 times – or some 50 per cent above the long-run average. The absolute peak in this valuation has typically come ahead of the top of the market itself, in one case as much as five years ahead, as Table 1.1 shows.

TABLE 1.1 – LOST ERA VALUATIONS

Peak valuation date	Peak long-term PE valuation	Lost era begins	Peak long-term dividend yield (%)
June 1901	25.2	September 1906	4.4
September 1929	32.6	September 1929	3.7
January 1966	24.1	December 1968	2.9
December 1999	44.2	July 2000	1.1

Source: Robert J. Shiller[8]

Overvaluation, then, seems to play a significant role in bringing about lost eras on Wall Street. And as we shall see shortly, lost eras tend to end once the stock market has become significantly undervalued. But are there any other common features that may cause lost eras?

Every one these of episodes since the early 1900s has played host to a major international conflict in which the United States was a leading combatant, namely the first and second world wars, the Vietnam War, and most recently, the conflicts in Afghanistan and Iraq.

While lost eras have tended to encompass major wars, this is not the same as saying that the conflicts caused those periods of poor stock returns. Both world wars and the War on Terror broke out unexpectedly and some time after the lost eras had begun. At the very most, therefore, it may have been the case that these conflicts deepened the stock market's difficulties in these periods. If so, there is one consequence of warfare in particular that could have hurt equities – *inflation*.

INFLATION

Times of war are almost invariably times of inflation. Rather than meeting the expense of the war effort by issuing bonds and raising taxes alone, governments typically resort to printing money and manipulating interest rates in order to keep them artificially low. The inevitable result of these tactics is persistently rising prices, especially when combined with the shortages of consumer goods that have usually occurred during the great conflicts of history. And inflation is one of the worst enemies of stock market returns over time.

There is a widespread misconception that equities always offer a hedge against inflation. It is said that because companies often have the power to raise their prices, corporate profits are therefore able to keep pace with inflation. In the long run, there may be some truth to this. But short bursts of high inflation are generally very harmful to the stock market. In the case of the US stock market, for example, real returns have always been negative in years where consumer prices have risen by more than six per cent.[9]

The link between inflation and lost eras becomes even clearer when we look more closely at the specific years in question. Since 1900, there have been 23 years where the US consumer price index rose by more than six per cent. All but one of those highly inflationary years occurred within lost eras for Wall Street. Not surprisingly, perhaps, all but three of these years came after the establishment of America's central bank, the Federal Reserve, in 1913.

THE FEDERAL RESERVE AND CENTRAL BANKS

Since inflation is largely a creation of the Fed and of central banks in general, at least some of the blame for lost eras must surely be laid at their door. It was mentioned earlier that Wall Street's two lost eras of the early 19th century came to an end far sooner than those of the modern era. One reason for this could be to do with the intervention of the Federal Reserve. Markets can adjust to the right level much more effectively when not subjected to meddling by governments.

This issue is more relevant today than ever before. The Federal Reserve responded to the onset of today's lost era in the early 2000s with near zero per cent interest rates, producing a 105 per cent bull market in stocks between 2003 and 2007. And its money-printing programmes since 2009 have helped deliver similarly impressive results, with the S&P also rising more than 100 per cent in an even shorter period of time. The danger, however, is that the Fed may simply be delaying the necessary bankruptcies and falls in asset prices. And, even if it succeeds in preventing these, it may only be doing so at a cost of creating stubbornly high inflation in the future, which would inevitably harm stocks.

How to cope with lost eras

While it is interesting to consider the reasons why lost eras happen, the most important question for us as investors is how we should deal with them. The first lesson of history is clear: we cannot simply rely on a buy-and-hold strategy to deliver the sort of returns to which we aspire during these periods. Annualised capital returns after inflation for the S&P 500 during the lost eras of the 20th century averaged *minus* 3.8 per cent.

All investors are aware, of course, that capital gains are only part of the story. To fully understand performance of equities during lost eras we also need to consider dividends and particularly the effect of reinvesting those dividends back into the market. Over extended periods, what really grows one's portfolio is the effect of reinvesting dividends received. The performance of all the stock markets of the developed world over time looks a great deal better once reinvested dividends are included. This is true even during lost eras; once reinvested dividends are included, the annualised real return during lost eras for the S&P 500 improves to *minus* 1.5 per cent. Even with this recalculated and improved performance, it is evident that a buy-and-hold approach is not wise during these lost eras.

So, what are investors to do?

Diversifying into emerging markets

Of course, there is no reason to remain exclusively invested in US stocks or those of any other single market. Today, more than ever before, we can get exposure to equities from far-off lands with ease. And the experience of previous lost eras suggests that we may indeed be well advised to consider doing so. While lost eras have often occurred in numerous markets simultaneously, some nations' equities have not only survived these periods better than others but have even prospered in absolute terms.

The Great Depression lost era of the 1930s initially saw concerted declines in stock markets around the world, as economic growth and international trade shrank alarmingly. However, some emerging equity markets of the day bounced back noticeably sooner and delivered much better returns. For example, stocks in Australia and New Zealand delivered an annualised real capital return of 3.5 and 2.2 per cent respectively from 1930 to 1940. By comparison, the S&P 500 made annualised real capital loss of minus 3.5 per cent a year in this period.[10]

A similar pattern emerges in Wall Street's lost era of 1968 to 1982. Asian stocks far outshone Western markets, including those of the US, UK and the larger continental European players. Japan – which was making the transition from emerging to developed market status around this time – achieved an annualised capital return before inflation in US dollar terms of 13.6 per cent, compared to 0.4 per cent for the S&P 500. Taiwan, meanwhile, generated an annualised return of 11 per cent and Hong Kong 18.1 per cent.

Getting access to emerging markets was much harder for Western investors in the past than it is today, even had they been adventurous and far-sighted enough to have wanted to do so. Whereas today's investors can easily speculate upon far-flung assets via exchange-traded funds that trade on their local stock exchange, no such products existed in the 1970s. Also, currency controls and other restrictions prevented many people from investing in anything beyond their home shores.

However, while we do now enjoy the freedom to invest in emerging markets as never before, there is one reason why this strategy may not work as well as it would have done a generation ago. The world economy and its many financial markets are much more closely intertwined than they were back in the 1970s. Barriers to trade have been pulled down, while capital flows across borders more or less unfettered. While these things are good for economic growth and for investor freedom, they also mean that stock markets are prone to move more closely together.

Happily, investing in emerging markets has paid off nicely during the latest lost era on Wall Street since 2000. From the turn of the new century to the end of 2011, the MSCI Emerging Markets Index – which tracks the performance of the stock markets of 26 emerging countries – went up by 47 per cent after inflation. The S&P 500 was down by 36 per cent in real terms over the same period.

At the worst moments of stress during today's lost era, however, emerging markets have actually fallen even more than Wall Street. Stocks in China, India and Brazil – three of the most exciting growth stories of our age – all underperformed the S&P in dollar-adjusted terms during the painful bear market between October 2007 and March 2009. In other words, diversifying into these exotic markets is an approach that can let us down at the precise times when we most require the benefits of diversification.

BONDS AND CASH

The best way to spread our equity risks during a lost era is clearly to look beyond the equity markets. As we saw at the beginning of this chapter, both US bonds and cash have proved much better investments since Wall Street entered its latest long-term funk. This is also the case in Japan, where investors have achieved excellent returns from holding long-term and short-term government bonds, despite record low yields on these assets.

In the 1930s, America, Britain, France and many other nations suffered from falling prices resulting from a massive collapse of debt. In this environment, the highest-quality bonds were among the clear winners. US government bonds produced a real return of seven per cent a year between 1930 and 1940. With the advent of the Second World War, inflation came roaring back in the US, as during every other major conflict. Bonds made an annualised loss of two per cent in that decade.

Much depends on the nature of the particular lost era as to whether bonds and cash prosper. The last lost era that ended in 1982 involved particularly fierce inflation. As such, longer-term US government bonds made an annualised loss after inflation of 1.7 per cent in the 1970s, while short-term bills suffered a decline on the same basis of 0.95 per cent a year.[11]

As of 2012, inflation has yet to become a serious problem in the US and much of the rest of the developed world. In fact, deflation is widely considered to be the more serious threat, hence central banks' pursuit of zero-interest rate policies and money-printing programmes. However, these things can change quite quickly. There are precedents for inflation following hot on the heels of deflation. It is not inconceivable, therefore, that we experience a lost era of two halves. If so, consider that deflation is usually good for bonds and cash investments while inflation negatively impacts the performance of these assets.

GOLD IN LOST ERAS

Despite inflation not yet having become a problem in the period since 2000, gold has been one of the strongest performers of the present lost era. Its price rocketed from $286 an ounce at the start of the new millennium to more than $1,925 by September 2011. This amounts to an annualised real return of some 13.7 per cent. Driving this stunning performance has been cheap money. When real interest rates fall, gold has typically come into its own.

Comparing gold's showing over recent years with how it did during Wall Street's previous lean spells is somewhat difficult. For most of the first seven decades of the 20th century, gold's price was essentially fixed by government decree, reflecting its historic use as backing for the US dollar and other currencies. Sizing up returns from holding gold during the lost eras of the 1910s and the Great Depression alongside those of more recent times is not entirely realistic, therefore.

However, gold did become freely traded around the outset of the last lost era for equities in 1968. And it famously proved to be an excellent investment during the inflationary years of the 1970s, hitting a then record high of $875 by early 1980, twenty-five times above its price of a decade earlier. As of early 2012, gold has yet to surpass its peak of 1980 in real terms, which in today's money equates to around $2,420. If the current lost era enters an inflationary phase, gold's chances of matching and surpassing that price seem very good.

SPOTTING THE END OF A LOST ERA

TO BUY-AND-HOLD INVESTORS, a lost era in stocks can seem like an eternity. However, these episodes do eventually come to an end. This clearly throws up an opportunity to earn significant returns, as anyone who was fortunate enough to have bought heavily into US stocks in the early 1920s, 1950s or 1980s would be able to attest. So, what might the end of today's lost era look like?

THE LENGTH OF LOST ERAS

In terms of time, Wall Street's current long-term losing spell has already lasted some 12 years as of early 2012. The shortest lost era of the modern age was just under 14 years, whereas the average over history is around 15 years. On this basis alone, there could be further lacklustre returns in store for US stocks and those of developed markets elsewhere.

EQUITY VALUATIONS

A more important clue is likely to come from equity valuations. We have seen how lost eras tend to begin with significant overvaluation in US stocks. They also come to an end after equities have become genuinely *under*valued. We take the end of a lost era to be when the next long-term uptrend begins. In each of the last three cases, the next long-term uptrend in the market has got underway when the S&P's cyclically-adjusted price-to-earnings ratio has dipped well into single digits. The data for this can be seen in Table 1.2. (The index traded on a multiple of 5.6 in 1932, although the next bull market did not start for another 17 years.)

TABLE 1.2 – VALUATIONS AT THE END OF LOST ERAS

Lost era end date	End valuation (long-term PE)	End valuation dividend yield
December 1920	4.8	6.1%
June 1949	9.1	6.2%
August 1982	6.6	6.4%

Source: Robert J. Shiller

Since its last great top in 2000, Wall Street has not come anywhere near to being as cheap as it was at the end of any previous lost era. When the S&P hit its lowest point to date in today's lost era, back in the dark days of 2009, it traded on a long-term price-to-earnings multiple of 13.3. This is more than double its average valuation at the end of previous lost eras. The same is true when we look at dividend yields, which have risen to above six per cent at the bottom in every previous lost era. The highest dividend yield registered since 2000 is a mere 3.2 per cent, by contrast.

A commonly heard argument from stockbrokers is that we will probably never again see such depressed valuations as were recorded at major lows in the past. After all, the Federal Reserve nowadays seems to regard propping up the stock market as part of its mandate – or at least as a highly desirable goal – and will therefore inject money into the market in hard times, keeping valuations permanently higher. These policies, however, risk stoking inflation, which would almost certainly ultimately undermine valuations.

The entire notion that long-term average valuations have become irrelevant in the modern age sounds uncomfortably similar to the sort of logic that was employed to justify past equity bubbles. One need only recall Professor Fisher's pronouncement that Wall Street had reached a "permanently high plateau" in 1929. For a present day case of how extreme valuations can revert to where they were in the past, we should look to Japan.

In the 1970s, the dividend yield on the Japanese stock market averaged around 2.2 per cent. Shortly after the stock market bubble burst in December 1989, the yield had been squeezed to a mere 0.4 per cent. While the yield remained below one per cent until late 2002, it has since returned sharply to pre-bubble levels.

PRICES OF BONDS, COPPER AND MARKET VOLATILITY

Besides valuation, there may be other signals we can look for to help determine that a lost era might finally be coming to an end. In his masterful study of the major bear markets of the 20th century, Russell Napier found that the prices of bonds, copper and investor activity can all provide pointers. Specifically, he shows that copper, government and corporate bonds all tend to make their final low and then turn upwards ahead of the stock market. He also advises watching out for a final slump in the stock market accompanied by low numbers of shares actually changing hands.[12]

THE PUBLIC MOOD

While asset prices and valuations give us much of what we need to determine when the balance has shifted too far against stocks, it is worth also monitoring more subjective evidence of the public's mood. In August 1979, towards the end of the last lost era, *Businessweek* magazine ran a cover story entitled 'The Death of

Equities', which bemoaned the poor outlook for stocks. It ended with a quote from a young executive: "Have you been to an American stockholders' meeting lately? They're all old fogies. The stock market is just not where the action's at."[13]

Joseph Kennedy – father of JFK and first chairman of America's Securities & Exchange Commission – is reputed to have sold his stock holdings in advance of the Great Crash beginning in 1929. He famously claimed to have been spooked into divesting himself of his portfolio when his shoe-shine boy started giving him stock-tips, a dead giveaway that the lowest echelons of the general public were becoming unthinkingly involved in the market.

An anecdotal sign that the present lost era has ended could well come when the subject of equities again becomes almost socially unacceptable.When we reach a point such as this it may well prove a good moment to renew one's faith in the cult of equity.

ENDNOTES

[1] Elroy Dimson, Paul Marsh, Mike Staunton, *Credit Suisse Global Investment Returns Sourcebook 2010*, p. 178.

[2] Jeremy Siegel, *Stocks for the Long Run* (McGraw-Hill Professional, 4th edition, 2008).

[3] Calculations made from stock market data set of Robert J. Shiller, originally published in *Irrational Exuberance* (Princeton University Press, 2000; Broadway Books, 2001; 2nd ed., 2005).

[4] I am grateful to Professors David Le Bris and Pierre-Cyrille Hautcoeur for letting me use their excellent recreation of the CAC 40 back to the mid-19th century.

[5] Elroy Dimson, Paul Marsh, Mike Staunton, *Credit Suisse Global Investment Returns Sourcebook 2010*, p. 90 and 163.

[6] Edward Chancellor, 'China's Red Flags', GMO Working Paper (March 2010), pp. 1-3.

[7] Calculation made from stock market data set of Robert J. Shiller, originally published in *Irrational Exuberance*.

[8] Data from the stock market data set of Robert J. Shiller, originally published in *Irrational Exuberance*.

[9] Calculations made from stock market data set of Robert J. Shiller, originally published in *Irrational Exuberance*.

[10] Dimson, Marsh, Staunton, *Global Investment Returns Sourcebook 2010*.

[11] Dimson, Marsh, Staunton, *Global Investment Returns Sourcebook 2010*, p.172.

[12] Russell Napier, *Anatomy of the Bear* (Harriman House, 2007).

[13] '*The Death of Equities*', Businessweek (13 August 1979).

CHAPTER 2

WILL DELEVERAGING DRAG US DOWN?

DELEVERAGING IS AN UGLY CONSTRUCT of a word. Mercifully, it is seldom heard outside of financial circles. But while the actual word may be alien to most lay folk, the process of deleveraging is touching everyone in some way today. Following the catastrophe of the credit crunch, the developed world has begun the long and painful task of reducing its enormous debt burden to more sustainable levels.

The deleveraging process promises to be one of the defining financial themes of the coming years. It will affect economic growth for the foreseeable future and perhaps our attitudes and behaviour for even longer. It could well also lead to the restriction of certain liberties that we currently enjoy, especially in relation to how we invest. We could therefore end up both less free and less wealthy.

WHAT INDEBTEDNESS INVOLVES

IF WE ARE TO PROTECT OURSELVES from the worst consequences of deleveraging, we first need a better understanding of what national indebtedness involves. There is still little agreement over how the process is likely to play out. Some argue the West could buckle under the weight of its over-indebtedness, suffering a prolonged period of stagnation and falling prices, as Japan has done for more than 20 years. Others believe that government efforts to ease the effects of debt crisis risk stoking runaway inflation.

The bald figures relating to today's indebtedness do seem mind-boggling. Close to Times Square in New York hangs a giant electronic ticker board that shows America's national debt, which updates itself in real time. As well as the US's gross debt figure, each citizen's share of the debt is displayed. (At the time of writing, the two figures were \$15,441,792,468,925 and \$49,447.17 respectively.) Debt clocks like these have proliferated on the internet in recent years and the numbers often find their way into the mainstream news headlines.

Economists typically compare a country's debt-load to the size of its economy. For example, if we add together the debts of America's government, its households and its companies, they come to around 3.5 times the size of the US economy as of early 2012.[14] While the US has the largest debts in absolute money terms, it is not the most leveraged. Among developed nations, both Japan and the United Kingdom have run up total borrowings of more than 4.5 times the size of their respective economies.

LEVELS OF LEVERAGE

The \$64 trillion dollar question, however, is how much leverage represents too much leverage. The ultimate risk of taking on too much debt is not being able to repay it, or at least meet interest payments upon it. This has been a depressingly regular phenomenon in emerging economies over the last two centuries. Carmen Reinhart, Kenneth Rogoff and Miguel Savastano have found that countries with a poor credit history can experience difficulties when the value of their obligations owed to foreigners rises to a mere 20 per cent of the size of their economies.[15]

Today's age of over-indebtedness extends far beyond serially-defaulting emerging-market countries. The mountains of debt stacked up in the US, UK and Japan would have crushed many emerging economies a very long time ago. Nevertheless, the governments of all three of these nations are still able to borrow at some of the lowest rates of any country at any time ever. It would be very dangerous, however, to assume that this situation can simply continue indefinitely.

Even while enjoying the lowest borrowing costs of any country in the world, Japan had to devote nearly half of the tax revenues that it received in 2011 to servicing its debts. Were the country's long-term borrowing costs to double from around one per cent to a slightly more normal level of two per cent or more, it clearly would face a serious squeeze, which would logically force it to reduce spending and perhaps also raise taxes. Cutting public spending would be difficult in Japan, with its rapidly ageing population. In addition, raising taxes could choke the country's chronically enfeebled economic growth.

IMPACT ON ECONOMIC GROWTH

Once government debt becomes unwieldy in relation to an economy's size, growth typically suffers. When gross public debt in an advanced economy is below 60 per cent, GDP growth averages 3.4 per cent a year, according to Reinhart and Rogoff's data. But when it rises above 90 per cent growth tends to shrink by a percentage point or more. For emerging markets, over-indebtedness can really start to take its toll on the growth of the economy at much lower levels of public debt, at around just 60 per cent.[16]

Still, the situation in developed countries has been much worse at certain times in the past than it is today. In the case of Britain, for example, net public indebtedness has averaged more than 100 per cent of the size of the economy over the very long term, as Chart 2.1 shows. Of course, the UK economy is very different now to what it was in the 19th century. Looking just at the 20th century, though, public indebtedness was evidently far above current levels for very long periods, but eventually came down without the country defaulting.

CHART 2.1 – UK PUBLIC NET DEBT AS A PERCENTAGE OF GDP, 1692 TO 2011

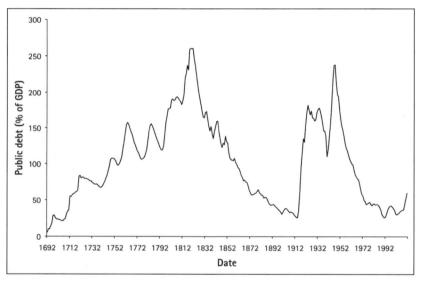

Data courtesy of **www.ukpublicspending.co.uk**

This cycle of leveraging up followed by deleveraging probably goes back beyond the time when formal records such as these begin. There is evidence of a debt cycle at work in the times of the Old Testament. The book of Leviticus (25:10) refers to a 'Jubilee Year' that was to be celebrated every half century, under which debts in ancient Israel were written off and land rights would be restored to their original owners.

THE CAUSE OF INDEBTEDNESS

THANKS IN PARTICULAR to the masterful database assembled by Professors Reinhart and Rogoff, we have a better idea than ever before about the cycle in debt over time. But what causes indebtedness to swell in the first place? Traditionally, government debts have tended to grow most noticeably as a result of the expense of fighting major wars. The big spikes in 20th century British government indebtedness, for example, reflected the enormous cost of fighting the two world wars in that century.

Although Britain and especially the United States have spent significant sums fighting the War on Terror since 2001, their respective national debts have lately risen mainly because of the financial crisis. The principal cost has been that of bailing out industries stricken by the credit crunch: the banking sector in the UK and the car-making, mortgage-lending and banking sectors in the US. This is also largely true for the many other countries across the developed world where public debt has spiralled since 2007.

HOUSEHOLD DEBT

Of course, government indebtedness is only one part of the problem today. Companies and households in numerous developed economies took on enormous amounts of debt in advance of the crisis. It is much harder to make sense of this debt-binge by comparing it to past episodes because data for private indebtedness going back in time is much scarcer than figures for government borrowing.

The debt-load of US households – for which we have some of the fullest data – has risen from just under a quarter of GDP in 1951 to a high of 101.6 per cent in late 2009. The long-term trend has clearly been towards ever-increasing amounts of personal debt, as can be seen in Chart 2.2. Britain, too, has seen households progressively take on more and more obligations over the long run.

And in very recent decades, consumers in Spain, France and South Korea have followed their lead.

Chart 2.2 – US Household debt as a percentage of GDP, 1951 to 2011

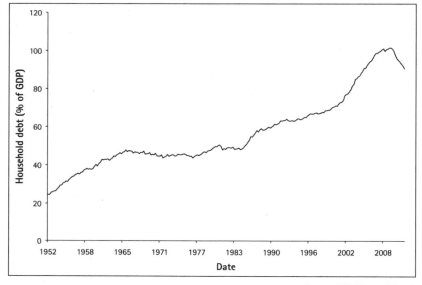

Source: US Flow of Funds

Large-scale household borrowing is most probably a modern phenomenon. Traditionally, personal indebtedness had a great deal of social stigma attached to it. In Victorian Britain – as well as in other societies around the world – those unable to pay their taxes, rent or debt could be thrown into debtors' prison. But even after the abolition of debtors' prison in 1869, social attitudes towards debt remained conservative and even disapproving well into the 20th century.

Private sector debt

While the data for the private sector may not be anything like as long and detailed as that for government borrowing, there is anecdotal evidence of corporate borrowing manias over time.

Writing in the 1930s, Professor Irving Fisher of Yale University alluded to regular debt-fuelled booms and busts in the US. These were centred upon real estate, cotton and transport in 1837, on railways and farming in 1873, and most famously, upon real estate, cars and radios in the early interwar years.[17]

As to the reasons behind these private debt-fuelled booms, Professor Fisher suggested that the most common was the perception of fresh opportunities to make a big profit. These included inventions, mineral discoveries or the opening up of previously closed or exotic markets. The other main cause he cited was easy money. If credit is cheap, he argued, people would be tempted to "borrow, invest and speculate."

AVAILABILITY OF CHEAP CREDIT

The view that loose money is to blame for the debt cycle seems particularly attractive in today's climate. The role of central banks and the wider banking system in causing the debt bubble and subsequent collapse has come under increasing scrutiny of late. As we discuss in Chapter 10, the central banks of the US, UK, Japan and the eurozone deliberately set interest rates at ultra-low levels in the early 21st century, but also in the period before then.

According to the Austrian school of economics, artificially low interest rates give misleading signals to businesses. As a result, investment projects are undertaken that would not have looked attractive had a more realistic rate of interest applied. This leads to money being *mal-invested*, in Austrian parlance, and to consequent overproduction of goods. Eventually, though, this becomes obvious and the debt machine goes into reverse gear.

When debt boom turns to debt bust

The switch from debt boom to debt bust is probably the least understood part of the process. For many years, companies and households seem content to amass ever increasing quantities of debt. And then, all of a sudden, their behaviour undergoes a sea-change. Lenders try to call in some of the loans they have made and borrowers seek to reduce their obligations.

An interesting – if very left-of-field – possibility comes from Robert J. Prechter, a pioneer of socionomics, or the study of social mood.[18] This school of thought argues that social mood is the driver of events rather than the other way round. Within this view, economic booms – and the debt build-ups that often accompany them – are caused by a positive mood in society, rather than the positive mood being caused by the rise in debt. Eventually, society's mood changes without any apparent trigger, whereupon a downturn occurs and debt is repaid.

Prechter's alternative explanation does raise a useful point about the lack of an obvious trigger. But perhaps we should look not for a single obvious trigger, such as a headline-grabbing bankruptcy or other economic shock, and instead focus on an unseen tipping-point within the investment process itself.

A useful concept here is that of a *Minsky moment*, derived from the work of the economist Hyman Minsky. In a boom, investors take on large debts to finance the purchase of speculative assets. A Minsky moment occurs when the cash flow on these assets proves insufficient to service the debts, which compels investors to liquidate and pay down their obligations. In 2007, for example, an increasing number of speculative real-estate investors in the US, UK and continental Europe were finding it hard to meet payments on their mortgages. This led to falling property prices and defaults, which badly hurt over-extended lenders too.

PSYCHOLOGICAL EFFECT ON SOCIETY

Just as the deleveraging process can dramatically impact the economy, it has been suggested that the experience of such an episode could have lasting psychological effects on society. Those born around the time of America's Great Depression in the interwar era were described in a legendary 1951 cover story in *Time* magazine as the "silent generation." They were characterised as "withdrawn, cautious, unimaginative, indifferent, unadventurous and silent." Part of this generational personality may have been the result of the lingering taste of hardship left from their childhood.

The habits gained from being raised in the crisis years of the 1930s stayed with many members of the silent generation for life. These included an insistence on mending old clothes rather than buying new ones and an aversion to borrowing to pay for consumption. Could it be that the credit-crunch generation will be affected likewise? A survey carried out in the UK in mid-2009, just as the country was emerging from its deepest slump since the Depression, showed that children as young as seven were picking up on their parents' financial worries and were thus proving less likely to pester them for toys.[19]

It is much too early to know whether such effects will turn out to be anything more than fleeting, but there seems to be a very strong chance that they will not. In the first place, parallels with the Depression era are seriously overdone. The economic collapse of 1930s was many times more severe across much of the world. The US economy, for example, shrank by 30 per cent between 1929 and 1932, while more than one in five people were out of work. By contrast, the US economy contracted by a mere five per cent from late 2007 to mid-2009 and unemployment hasn't gone much above one in ten.

Even for those worst affected by today's debt collapse, the experience has been markedly different to that of the Great Depression's worst victims. Welfare provision in the 1930s was minimal or non-existent in most developed countries. Some unemployed Americans were reduced to living in shanty-towns and relied on charitable organisations for food. By contrast, unemployed welfare recipients in contemporary Britain and elsewhere often enjoy a more comfortable existence than those in low-paid work.

Of necessity, the heavily-hocked consumers of the US and UK have paid down some of their personal borrowings in recent years. Outstanding credit card debt in America went down in 32 of 37 months to November 2011. Unsecured consumer lending in Britain shrank four per cent to £217bn in 2011.[20] However, paying down debt in difficult-times is hardly proof of any deep and lasting cultural rejection of borrowing.

What is more, consumerism remains now deeply rooted in both developed and emerging societies. Advertising has never been more sophisticated or more intense than it is today. The desire to own designer accessories and hi-tech gadgetry therefore is as strong as ever. In October 2011, as both America and Britain appeared to be flirting with recession once more, shoppers all over the country queued for hours outside Apple stores in order to be among the first to own the latest version of its iPhone, at a cost of several hundred dollars each. Contrast this to the Great Depression era, when people queued for hours for food.

OFFICIAL MANAGEMENT OF THE CRISIS

Official efforts to manage the aftermath of the credit crisis may also influence people's attitudes to debt in years to come. In the early 1930s, many developed nations' governments responded to the slump by immediately trying to run strictly balanced budgets and keeping their currencies rigidly fixed to gold. The contemporary response has been the exact opposite. The authorities have increased their indebtedness with stimulus measures and banking bailouts, while trying to create inflation via money-printing.

This is much more than just a question of economic policy-differences. The governments' handling of these two crises contained implicit moral messages. In the 1930s, the emphasis on balanced budgets and sound money was an official endorsement of thrift and taking responsibility. Today's cocktail of bailouts and inflationary measures entails largesse in favour of companies and individuals that have made bad decisions.

The massive state assistance given to the financial industry across Europe and in the US has already proved highly controversial. Economists have warned that it risks creating a "moral hazard" problem, wherein bankers will be tempted to lend and speculate even more recklessly in the future, in the belief that governments will again bail them out if things go wrong. This surely applies equally to the general public. Seeing taxpayers' money used to support already privileged groups could reinforce an implicit belief that irresponsible behaviour pays off.

What governments now do to reduce the enormous debts that they have built up over recent years could also profoundly influence society's future attitudes towards debt. Several years after the credit crisis erupted, there is still a vigorous debate concerning exactly how deleveraging will play out, with much more at stake than mere intellectual kudos. The winning side should also end up a great deal financially better off than the losing side.

HOW INDEBTEDNESS CAN BE REDUCED

THERE ARE THREE MAIN WAYS that society's debt burden can come down over time. First, the economy can experience real growth, which reduces the relative size of the debt and also allows debt to be repaid. Another possibility is that the size of the economy is artificially grown by way of inflation, while the debt remains fixed. Alternatively, debtors can renegotiate or even default upon their obligations.

These various choices are not mutually exclusive. As an economy grows naturally, some inflation usually occurs too, thus shrinking the debt in two ways simultaneously. There will also likely be some shrinkage of the debt from defaults and restructurings even if growth and inflation are in evidence. However, deleveraging periods are usually dominated by one of these three forces in particular.

The optimal outcome is if the economy experiences genuine growth in order to ease its debt-burden. This can be a tall order in cases where debt is especially heavy, as the research of Reinhart and Rogoff has so ably demonstrated. In cases of heavy indebtedness, the natural tendency is often towards a deflationary collapse. The classic example of this was the Great Depression of the 1930s.

Shortly after the 1929 to 1932 meltdown, Irving Fisher explained a deflationary debt-collapse in terms of a chain of consequences. First, investors seek to pay off debt *en masse*, resulting in distress-selling. In turn, this leads to shrinking bank credit and a falling stock of money. Prices then fall, squeezing profits and the value of assets. Trade contracts and businesses lay off workers, leading to lower confidence all round and money-hoarding. As prices fall, interest costs effectively rise.

The science of economics has become more sophisticated since Fisher's time, but his basic message still resonates. "It is always economically possible to stop or prevent such a depression simply by reflating the price level up to the average level at which outstanding debts were contracted by existing debtors and assumed by existing creditors, and then maintaining that level unchanged," he wrote.[21] This logic has inspired the money-printing or *quantitative easing* exercises that central banks in the West have pursued in response to the latest crisis.

DELEVERAGING THROUGH INFLATION

ALTHOUGH QUANTITATIVE EASING is not a new idea, the scale of these efforts over recent years has been unprecedented. Between 2008 and 2011, America's Federal Reserve created more than $2 trillion out of thin air, which it has used in order to buy up US government bonds and other assets, and thereby pump money into the financial system. The Bank of England (BoE) was even more zealous in its approach, such that it owned an astonishing one-third of the total UK government bonds in issue as of early 2012.

Despite the enormous debts weighing down upon both the US and UK economies, deflation has so far largely been avoided. Although consumer price growth fleetingly turned negative in both countries in 2009, inflation rates have since turned positive again. In the UK, indeed, where the central bank's money-printing has been most aggressive, annual growth in the Retail Price Index actually reached an uncomfortably high rate of 5.1 per cent in 2011.

THE EXAMPLE OF 1946

We only have to look back a few decades for the last case of developed-world governments deleveraging by way of inflation. It is worth our decomposing what exactly happened in some detail here. The US emerged from the Second World War with Federal debts of $271bn in 1946 – equivalent to 122 per cent of GDP. This leverage shrank progressively over the coming decades, reaching a post-war low of 31.8 per cent in 1981.[22]

The US did pay off some of its $271bn debt immediately after the war – some $19bn of it by 1948, to be precise. However, the Federal debt then rose in all but four years leading up to 1981. Even in those four years, the biggest one-year decline in the debt was just 0.8 per cent. Since America did not default on any of its liabilities, post-war deleveraging in America therefore came about entirely by other means.

The two most important factors in this deleveraging process were economic growth and inflation. Between 1950 and 1981, the US economy grew from $275bn to $3,195bn – an increase of 1,061 per cent. Stripping out inflation, however, the economy grew by just 211 per cent.[23] Inflation was therefore much the more important influence in accomplishing deleveraging at this time.

The world's largest economy was not an exception in this period. It has become the norm in the modern world for countries to manage their indebtedness over time by way of creating inflation. The ability to print one's own currency at will is the key to this. Such tactics were much harder in the era before the Second World War, when many nations' currencies were tied to gold. Inflation is therefore an essential tool to governments today and one that they would be loath to give up, and especially just now.

HOLDING INTEREST RATES BELOW THE RATE OF INFLATION

A key element within a government inflating away debts is ensuring that interest rates are held below the rate of inflation. This helps to reduce the real value of existing debt and also keeps down the cost of new borrowing. To give just one example, the British government's long-term borrowing rate was below the UK RPI inflation rate in 23 of 25 months between 2010 and early 2012. Real bond yields also turned negative in that period in the US.

The intention to deleverage by way of inflation in both these highly indebted nations today could hardly be clearer. Oddly enough, however, there are still plenty of people who believe that the West is destined to experience a long period of stagnation accompanied by falling prices, just as Japan has done for the best part of 20 years. To support their argument, they cite the ultra-low yields on US, UK and German government bonds, which, they say, prove how dreadful the outlook for growth is.

There is an element of a truth to the case that weak economic growth has contributed to the very low bond yields seen between 2007 and 2012. But the picture is, of course, hugely distorted by the unprecedented buying of bonds by central banks, whose express intention is to keep bond yields at rock-bottom levels. This makes it hard to determine exactly where bond prices and yields would otherwise be – conveniently so for the authorities.

Given governments' long and shameful record of trying to unburden themselves of debt by way of monetary manipulation, we must consider the question of why investors would continue to hold government bonds in the coming years, especially once inflation becomes more of a stubborn problem. The likeliest answer is because some investors are already literally forced to own government debt – and may have even less choice in matters going forward.

FINANCIAL REPRESSION

FINANCIAL REPRESSION was a concept first popularised by Edward Shaw and Ronald McKinnon, two Stanford University professors in the 1970s. It describes the process by which the state intervenes in the credit market to manipulate credit flows for its own benefit. For example, a heavily indebted government might set interest rates lower than the rate of inflation. It might then oblige domestic investors to lend to it by preventing them by law from investing abroad.[24]

This process of financial repression leads significant amounts of government debt to be wiped out over time. A 2011 paper by Carmen Reinhart and M. Belen Sbrancia estimated the UK and US had liquidated debt equivalent to 3.4 per cent of GDP annually between 1945 and 1980.[25] Aside from keeping interest rates below the rate of inflation, the key instruments of financial repression are currency controls, limits on the rates that banks offer on savings and laws obliging institutional investors to hold certain amounts of government debt.

Investors have enjoyed steady increases in financial freedom over the decades since 1980. Inflation was generally below the rates available on cash savings and government bonds during the period until 2010, enabling investors to earn decent real returns on those assets. As such, governments in the developed world were content to relax many of the restrictions that they had previously placed on which products and where their citizens could invest.

Until 1980, for example, British investors were severely constrained when it came to investing beyond these shores. Even holidaymakers were only allowed to convert a tiny sum of pounds into other currencies to take abroad, for which privilege they required a special stamp in their passport. Today, of course, we can effortlessly invest anywhere in the world and in almost anything we please, wiring money instantly to a brokerage account in a far-flung country. It may therefore seem hard to imagine a return to strictures of the 1970s.

A lot of the coming repression in the developed world will inevitably target banks and pension funds. These institutions are compelled to hold certain amounts of government bonds in order to meet capital adequacy rules. As of 2012, such institutions are proving willing buyers of these instruments. The European Central Bank (ECB) is lending many hundreds of billions of Euros to commercial banks, which those banks are heavily using to add to their holdings of government bonds.

This is all well and good in a time of nervousness when banks are actually keen to shore up their asset-bases by holding more government bonds. When inflation becomes a problem later on, however, the proposition may seem less attractive. Governments may then resort to requiring banks and other institutions to hold even more of their bonds and may even forbid them from holding more appealing alternatives.

Such measures are not, of course, merely restrictions on giant corporations. It is the general public – the customers of those banks and pension funds – who ultimately suffer from financial repression. For financial repression to work the freedom of individuals to invest as they please will almost certainly have to be curtailed too. While we may not realise it, the devices required to enforce restrictions are steadily and quietly being put in place all around us.

HOW FINANCIAL REPRESSION CAN BE ENFORCED

Advances in technology since the last age of financial repression 30 years ago would make repressive measures easier to enforce today. The banking system is much more heavily computerised, with virtually all payments now executed electronically. This would make it much more practical for the authorities to keep tabs on activity and ensure the new restrictions were not circumvented.

At the same time, financial rules are more harmonised internationally and more strictly enforced than ever. Banks and other institutions are obliged to report transactions proactively to the authorities. Proving the source of one's funds for any significant investment like buying real estate is now mandatory in many places. Lots of these changes have been introduced in the name of anti-money laundering, especially in relation to the War on Terror.

Unbeknown to most people, European law already provides for controls to be imposed on capital flows between the European Union and the rest of the world. The European Commission has the power to take *protective measures* – i.e. exchange controls – when a member country is faced with a balance of payments crisis.[26] Past experience of such situations has shown repeatedly that supposedly temporary measures can very easily become permanent.

Deception is a further device in governments' arsenal of financial-repression weaponry, and one that is already being deployed. While US consumer price inflation has apparently stayed low in recent times, there is cause for doubt about the credibility of this figure.

The CPI has undergone many changes over the years, affecting everything from its overall approach right down to the finer details of how it is calculated. The official intention of these many alterations has been to make the CPI more representative of reality.

Sceptics retort that the underlying purpose behind variations to the CPI is to suppress the truth rather than promote it. The website Shadow Government Statistics (**www.shadowstats.com**) challenges key elements of much US government data and offers its own rival calculations. Were inflation in 2012 calculated in the same way that it was in 1990, maintains the site's creator, it would be above six per cent rather than below three per cent.

Official rigging of statistics may be still only a matter of opinion when it comes to the US, but it is a matter of fact elsewhere. China routinely cooks its books to suit the ruling Communist Party's political ends. Greece secured entry to the single European currency club by deliberately understating the size of its deficit. The Kirchener regime in Argentina massively under-reports inflation and harasses local statisticians who dare to contradict its version of events. It is hardly a stretch of the imagination to think that this could occur in the most advanced economies too, if the stakes were high enough.

FORMULATING INVESTMENT STRATEGY

IF DELEVERAGING CONTINUES down its present inflationary path over the coming years, as seems almost inevitable, we need to formulate our investment strategy accordingly. We already have a fairly good idea from the financial history of the last two centuries and more which assets are better placed to survive and even prosper in an environment of persistently rising prices and which are not.

While the prices of US, UK and Japanese government bonds remain near record highs as of early 2012, these bonds and others are among the likeliest obvious losers of the years ahead. The deleveraging of the post-war era saw heavy losses incurred on government and corporate bonds. The 1946 to 1981 period has been described as the "greatest of all secular bear bond markets" for the US, during which a constant maturity 30-year government bond would have lost 83 per cent of its value.[27]

The stock market is widely believed to provide a good hedge against inflation. This is somewhat true when it comes to steady inflation over time, but not so when it comes to shorter, high bursts of it. While equities fared better than bonds during the post-war age of deleveraging by inflation as a whole, they were hit hard during the runaway price growth in the 1970s and early 1980s. Historically, once America's consumer-price inflation rate has risen above six per cent, the US stock market has always tended to deliver a negative real annual return.

By contrast, many commodities boomed when inflation last became a problem. Gold and other precious metals are particularly well known for their ability to hold their value in an environment of unbridled inflation. These assets have enjoyed a fantastic boom since the dawn of the new millennium. But even though investors have already bid them up substantially, they stand to flourish further if real interest rates remain negative for some time, as seems probable.

Identifying desirable and undesirable investments for the rest of this age of deleveraging may be the easier part of the game. The biggest challenge of all could be executing our ideas as financial repression intensifies. Doing what is right for our capital could easily risk falling foul of the law in certain circumstances so having access to the deftest tax and legal advisers could soon become every bit as important as hiring the smartest fund manager.

ENDNOTES

[14] US Federal Reserve, Flow of Funds Accounts of the United States.

[15] Carmen Reinhart, Kenneth Rogoff and Miguel Savastano, 'Debt intolerance', MPRA Paper No. 13932, (March 2003).

[16] Carmen M. Reinhart, Kenneth S. Rogoff, 'Growth in a Time of Debt', *American Economic Review: Papers and Proceedings* (January 2010).

[17] The Debt-Deflation Theory of Great Depressions, Irving Fisher, Econometrica, 1933.

[18] Robert Prechter, Conquer the Crash: You Can Survive and Prosper in a Deflationary Depression (John Wiley & Sons, 2009).

[19] Credit crunch hits 'I want' generation – The Scotsman, 11 July 2009.

[20] US Federal Reserve, G.19 statistical report; UK Debt statistics from Credit Action, February 2012.

[21] Irving Fisher, 'The Debt-Deflation Theory of Great Depressions', *Econometrica* (1933).

[22] Figures courtesy of **www.usgovernmentdebt.us**

[23] US Federal Reserve, Flow of Funds Accounts of the United States.

[24] **www.stanford.edu/~mckinnon**

[25] Carmen M. Reinhart, M. Belen Sbrancia, 'The Liquidation of Government Debt', National Bureau of Economic Research Working Paper 16893.

[26] Nigel Foster, *Blackstone's EC Legislation 2006-2007*, 17th edition, p. 32.

[27] Sidney Homer and Richard Sylla, *A History of Interest Rates* (Wiley Finance, 4th edition, 2005).

CHAPTER 3

GOLD'S GLITTERING PATH

WESTFIELD SHOPPING CENTRE in West London is a temple of contemporary consumerism. Almost every conceivable material need and desire is catered for within its more than 300 individual stores. Prada garments and other exclusive designer goods are offered within 'the Village', the mall's swish VIP zone. Away from this plush enclave, shoppers can purchase anything from lingerie to teeth whitening, tacos to hydrotherapy.

You can also buy gold at Westfield. Apart from an impressive selection of jewellery, watches and pens sold in the shops, the yellow metal can be acquired there for investment purposes. In an undistinguished corner of the mall, alongside a cashpoint and a soft drinks-dispenser, is a rather special vending machine. This digital contraption offers a glittering array of golden goods, from a one-gram wafer to a bar weighing one-quarter of a kilo, with prices refreshed every ten minutes in line with the official London market price.

While the vending machine itself may rightly be regarded as something of a gimmick, the trend towards investing in gold seems to be anything but a passing fad. The price of gold has risen steadily from a low of $253 an ounce in 1999 to an all-time record high of $1,925 in the autumn of 2011 – a gain of 661 per cent. Over the same period, the total return on the MSCI World index of stocks was 20.9 per cent and that on a ten-year US government bond was 121 per cent.[28]

For the love of gold

HUMAN FONDNESS FOR HOLDING wealth in the form of gold goes back for literally thousands of years. The earliest gold coins were struck in the 7th century BC in what is now the Western part of Turkey and the use of gold as a store of value goes back even further still. Over the subsequent millennia, this metal has played a more enduring role in money and savings than perhaps any other individual asset.

Thanks to its long and illustrious history, gold today enjoys a following among some investors that verges upon cult adoration. To hear the metal's true believers on the subject, you would be forgiven for thinking it possessed supernatural properties. It is regularly touted as being the "only true form of money", offering protection in times of both inflation and deflation, as well as during wars, panics and natural disasters.

There are, of course, also a good few heretics who decry gold at every opportunity. Among other things, gold has been cast variously as a "barbarous relic" whose former use as money stunted economic growth and needlessly deepened depressions, and a device of sinister and shadowy forces who seek world domination. Some of its critics dismiss its recent gains as mindless speculation that is doomed to end in disaster.

Neither adulation nor abhorrence is of much help in determining the really important issue of what part gold should play in our investment strategies over the coming years. Instead, we should re-examine gold's performance over time and particularly its relationship to other assets. In light of this, we can then decide the likely outlook for gold – and also how best to own this metal. We will come to this later in the chapter, but we should start by looking at the relationship of gold to inflation.

GOLD AND INFLATION

BESIDES ITS ELEGANT LUSTRE, perhaps the most attractive property of gold is its scarcity. Only 165,000 metric tonnes of the stuff have been extracted from the earth throughout the whole of history, according to the World Gold Council.[29] Were this entire amount melted together into a single super-nugget, it would measure just 20 metres cubed. The total supply of gold only grows slowly, nowadays by around 1.5 per cent each year.

The scarcity of gold is in stark contrast to today's abundance of paper money. Since the onset of the credit crunch in 2007, central banks around the world have created new currency at an unprecedented rate in an effort to keep the badly-damaged financial system functioning. In the US alone, M2 – a measure of the money supply – ballooned from $7.4 trillion in June 2007 to $9.8 trillion at the start of 2012 – an increase of one-third. Even supporters of these policies acknowledge the risk of them stoking inflation at some point.

Gold's relationship with inflation over time is the subject of quite a lot of confusion – and perhaps more than a bit of deliberate misinformation. Chart 3.1 shows the price of gold and the US consumer price index (CPI) going back to the year 1801, with both rebased to 1. As of February 2012, the price of gold had gone up almost 90 times, whereas the consumer prices had gone up 18.5 times over the same period. It is therefore true that gold has more than kept up with one measure of inflation over the very long term.

CHART 3.1 – GOLD AND US INFLATION 1801 TO 2011

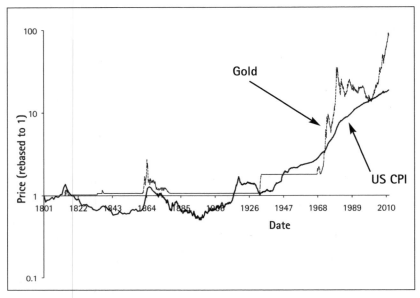

Source: *Investors Chronicle*, Robert Shiller

It is totally false, however, to say that gold has always gone up alongside inflation. US consumer prices rose modestly but steadily in the 1980s and 1990s, at an average of 4.3 per cent a year. But the price of gold actually fell in more than half of the years in that period. This represents a fairly long period, then, during which investors who put their faith in the yellow metal in order to protect themselves against inflation would have been sorely disappointed.

A popular retort of gold bugs at this point is that gold really comes into its own when faced with shorter bursts of stubbornly high inflation. The classic episode was that of the late 1960s and 1970s, when inflation got out of hand across much of the developed world and beyond. As the rate of US inflation galloped ahead to more than ten per cent a year by the end of the 1970s, gold's performance did indeed glisten, rising eight-fold from late 1976 to January 1980. Its price then collapsed once the Fed and other central banks got tough on inflation.

However, it would be hard to attribute gold's bull market in the early 21st century to inflation. Between summer 1999 and January 2012, America's CPI has averaged a very modest 2.5 per cent and has exceeded five per cent in just two months. It even turned mildly negative for much of 2009. Inflation has been similarly restrained across much of the rest of the world too, including in the heart of the eurozone, Switzerland and the UK. Japan, meanwhile, has suffered falling prices.

THE RELATIONSHIP BETWEEN INTEREST RATES AND INFLATION

The critical fact here is not the simple presence of inflation itself, but whether investors are properly compensated for that inflation or not. In the 1970s, inflation persistently ran above interest rates in many countries. In the US, for example, the annual rate of increase in the CPI outstripped the return available on three-month Treasury Bills more than 90 per cent of the time from 1974 to 1980. Savers who lent to the government were thus consistently punished for doing so.

As we have already seen, this unfortunate situation was totally reversed in the 1980s and 1990s. US Treasury Bills offered an interest rate ahead of inflation 94 per cent of the time. So, while there was persistent – albeit mainly moderate – inflation, savers and holders of government debt were properly compensated. During this period, gold lost more than two-thirds of its value – and even more in terms of its purchasing power.

Although gold reached its nadir in the summer of 1999, it was not until May 2001 that it really started to rally in a sustained way. That date is no coincidence, being precisely the time when inflation again started to get ahead of interest rates in America. US Treasury Bills offered a yield lower than inflation more than half the time in the 11 years after 2001, and increasingly so from late 2007.

HYPERINFLATION

The most extreme variety of inflation – and potentially therefore of uncompensated inflation – is hyperinflation. Sometimes defined as a situation where inflation rises at a rate equal to 100 per cent over three years, hyperinflation is often cited by gold bugs as a specific scenario against which gold would offer protection in the years ahead. The experiences of several countries that have suffered this scourge seem to bear this notion out.

Among the freshest examples, Zimbabwe was struck by hyperinflation in the first decade of the 21st century. By late 2008, inflation in Zimbabwe had soared to 500 billion per cent[30], whereas interest rates had only risen to around 1000 per cent, an obvious case of massively uncompensated inflation. Tellingly, Zimbabweans who held gold during that period would have been insulated from the runaway prices. The US dollar, in which gold is priced, soared versus the local Zimbabwean dollar, and was widely used as day-to-day currency and a store of value.

DEFLATION

Advocates of gold also frequently claim that it offers refuge during times of deflation or falling prices. Historically speaking, this is entirely correct. There were long spells of deflation in America during the 19th century, during which gold's purchasing power increased substantially. The same was true during the Great Depression era of the early 1930s. The purchasing power of an ounce of gold increased by 112 per cent from the eve of Wall Street Crash of 1929 until the outbreak of war in Europe in 1939.

Unfortunately, statistics like these are all but meaningless. During all of those historical episodes of deflation in the US, gold was actually a form of money, whose price was essentially set by government decree. In 1929, for instance, an ounce of gold was fixed at $20.67 per ounce. Its price remained fixed at $20.67 as consumer prices fell, meaning that its purchasing power had grown. Then, suddenly in 1933, the US government decreed that the price of gold was now $35/oz. Overnight, gold's purchasing power had risen by a further two-thirds.

Gold's link with paper money is now obviously a thing of the distant past. It was President Nixon in 1970 that finally severed the relationship between the US dollar and the yellow metal. Since the price of gold today is determined by market forces, therefore, it is surely misleading to look back to periods where it had direct use as currency, and when its price was typically frozen for decades at a time, for lessons about its performance.

Although historical gold prices may not be of any help in determining how it would behave were a major deflationary crisis to erupt today, there is still an argument that it might prosper. Deflationary crises are typically the result of the collapse of debt-fuelled bubbles. As it becomes clear that many borrowers – perhaps including some governments – are going to default on their debts, investors lose faith in paper money and seek alternative safe-havens to holding cash. In those conditions, gold could be a refuge of choice.

The main reason why people might lose faith in paper currency in a full-blown episode of deflation is to do with the likeliest official response to falling prices. Central banks in the Western world today are petrified of deflation. As consumer prices turned negative in America during the first ten months of 2009, the Federal Reserve reacted by conjuring up more than a trillion dollars, which it used to buy up various loans and also government bonds.

The Fed's buying spree began in November 2008, while deflation was still feared rather than actually present. At that point, the price of gold had dropped by one-third from its then all-time high of $1,034 in March of that year. But once the Fed showed what it was willing to do in order to avert persistently falling prices in the economy, gold started to rally impressively. Within three months, it was back near its previous record peak.

Thanks to the Fed's actions, the experience of deflation in 2009 was short-lived. Having gone below zero in January, the annual rate of CPI inflation turned positive again from November and remained so thereafter. But this is really far too short a period of deflation for us to draw any sound conclusions. Japan, by contrast, has suffered from persistently falling prices ever since the 1990s. Having suffered a brief bout of inflation in 1995, the problem became entrenched from early 1999.

The worst of the Japanese deflation coincides neatly with gold's bull market. In local-currency terms, the price of gold was ¥33,143 per ounce at the start of 1999. Over the next thirteen years, consumer prices fell around three-quarters of the time. The price of gold, however, enjoyed a great run over this period, reaching ¥140,410 by early 2012, an increase of 324 per cent. It did especially well in 2002 and 2005, both times as consumer prices were dropping at an accelerated pace.

Just because gold has boomed at a time of deflation in Japan, it clearly cannot be said that deflation is the cause of that boom, though. There is no evidence that the Japanese people have rushed to buy in gold at any time in recent years. In fact, the opposite is true. The country was estimated to have been a net seller of gold in 2010, to the tune of 78 tonnes. Japanese households have mainly responded to deflation by purchasing bonds from their own government and by holding cash in the bank.

GOLD IN TIMES OF TURMOIL

UNSTABLE PRICES – whether in the form of inflation or deflation – have the power to strike fear into investors' hearts. But they are not the only forces that do so. Financial markets often suffer understandable bouts of nervousness when faced with war, political instability and natural disasters, among other things. Popular wisdom has it that gold makes the ideal investment in such times.

This attitude towards gold was best summed up by Jim Slater, a famous British speculator, during the crisis of 1974. At the time, the UK was paralysed by strikes and rampant inflation, while a deeply socialist government bent on taxing the rich had just come to power. Amidst the chaos, there were even faint rumblings of military coup. Mr Slater famously advised people to consider buying "a bicycle, a shotgun, a supply of tinned baked beans and Krugerrands."[31]

There is no doubt that gold has proved a vitally important holding in certain particularly extreme situations. Jewish refugees who managed to escape Nazism in the 1930s and 1940s typically lost their businesses and homes for little or no compensation, but there were a few who are known to have owned gold coins or bars that they carried with them when they fled.

PERFORMANCE IN RECENT MOMENTS OF TENSION

Gold's performance in recent episodes of high tension does seem fairly solid. Table 3.1 shows gold's performance around some of the most dramatic international incidents of the last few decades.

TABLE 3.1 – PERFORMANCE OF GOLD DURING DRAMATIC INTERNATIONAL INCIDENTS

	Soviet invasion of Afghanistan 1979	Chernobyl 1986	Black Monday 1987 stock market crash	Kuwait invasion 1990	Attack on America, 2001	US invades Iraq, 2003	Japanese earthquake, 2011
Performance from ten days before to ten days after	39.8%	0.61%	2.8%	11.12%	5.64%	-5.39%	2.38%

Source: Datastream

The performance around the Soviet invasion of Afghanistan is especially eye-catching, but this is somewhat misleading, as gold was already in the final, frenetic stages of a speculative bubble at that time. Still, gold was definitely a useful holding during the worst ever single day's stock market crash in 1987 and also when Saddam Hussein attacked Kuwait in 1990.

The defining such event of our generation was the 9/11 terrorist attack on the US. Once financial markets reopened after the atrocity, risky assets like stocks collapsed dramatically. By contrast, gold surged from $274 on 10 September to a high of $296 a few days later. As investors recovered their nerve, gold gave back its gains, but then rose relentlessly from December 2001.

Of course, the very nature of events like these is that they typically come out of the blue; one can hardly plan to buy gold immediately ahead of them. The best solution, therefore, is to make gold a permanent fixture among our investment holdings. That makes especially good sense in light of gold's relationship to other assets, and to the stock market in particular.

GOLD'S PERFORMANCE VERSUS THAT OF OTHER ASSETS

EQUITIES

SINCE GOLD BECAME FREELY traded in 1968, it has often had a very weak or even negative relationship to equities. Chart 3.2 shows the twelve-monthly correlation between the metal and the S&P 500 over the entire period. A correlation of 1 suggests that the two prices move perfectly together, whereas a correlation of -1 suggests they move in totally the opposite way.

CHART 3.2 – ROLLING 52-WEEK CORRELATION BETWEEN GOLD AND THE S&P 500, 1968 TO 2011

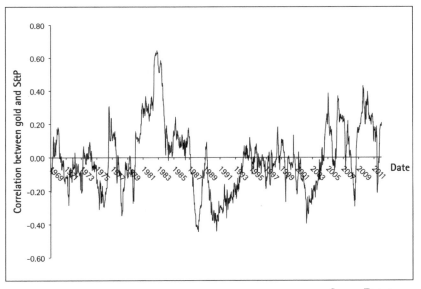

Source: Datastream

Seldom has the correlation between gold and the US stock market been stronger than 0.4. In fact, more often that not, the correlation has actually been negative. This relationship makes gold a great asset for balancing out risks on equity investments and vice versa.

A common criticism of gold is that it has achieved much worse returns than equities over the long run. A dollar invested in worldwide equities in 1900 would have grown to $344 after inflation by the end of 2011.[32] But $1 invested in gold would have become just $2.78 in real terms. The main reason for equities' vastly superior performance is the effect of reinvesting the dividend income that they generate. Gold, on the other hand, generates no income and instead actually costs money to store.

CURRENCIES

As well as considering how gold moves with stocks, we need to think about its relationship with currencies. Its most important relationship is that with the world's most important paper currency, the US dollar. Since both became freely traded a few decades ago, they have typically moved in the opposite direction to one another. A weaker dollar has generally been associated with a stronger gold price and vice versa. This poses us with a conundrum, especially if we wish to buy gold because we are fearful about the decline of the US dollar.

On the one hand, gold offers good insurance against a declining US dollar. On the other, the profits on our insurance policy will be paid out in a devalued currency. This is clearly a particularly important issue if the dollar is not our own home currency. For example, gold soared from $257 in early 2001 to around $1,000 in early 2008 – a gain of 289 per cent – but a European investor who correctly bought and then sold at these times would have made only 126 per cent in euro terms.

There may well be a case for hedging our exposure to the US dollar when we buy gold therefore. Currency hedging can be a fiddly business, but some gold-tracking products come with this feature automatically built in nowadays. For example, a British investor can buy a London-stock market listed gold ETF that is denominated in sterling, which also has physical gold backing. He is therefore protected against currency risk and also has the reassurance of owning something directly linked to actual gold rather than derivative contracts.

DESPITE GOLD'S LONG-TERM failure to keep up with equities, and the risk and difficulty of using gold to hedge currency movements, it can still prove superior to other asset classes for substantial periods, just as it has done in the 21st century to date. The main issue for investors as of early 2012 is to determine whether it can extend this performance over the coming years.

HOW GOLD WILL PERFORM IN THE YEARS AHEAD

THERE ARE QUITE A FEW CYNICS who believe that gold has already risen far too high and risks coming back down to earth with a bump, a process that may even have already begun.

Anecdotally, there are hints that the gold-rush of recent years may have got ahead of itself. Widespread public enthusiasm for an asset that has already gone up massively has often spelled trouble in the past. And what better sign of broad public enthusiasm could we have than gold-vending machines in shopping malls and airports or hugely popular exchange-traded funds? Also, the 30 per cent spike in the price of gold to a new record high between July and September 2011 had a slight whiff of panic-buying about it.

Although this sort of popular enthusiasm is a typical feature of the late stages of a boom, it is not sufficient in itself to signal an imminent bust. Nor does the price action of summer 2011 really qualify as irrational exuberance by past standards. In the final three months leading to gold's then record peak of 1980 – and its subsequent crash – its price jumped by 135 per cent.

We have already established that uncompensated inflation has been the main force driving gold over the last few decades. The outlook for inflation – and for interest rates – is therefore also likely to hold the key to its performance over the coming years. As I argue in Chapter 2, the governments of the developed world have already made a deliberate choice to generate uncompensated inflation in order to ease the burden of their heavy indebtedness.

This process of inflating away the debt has probably only just begun. America's Federal debt in 2011 was equivalent to 98.7 per cent of the size of the US economy, which is universally deemed to be much too high. The average between 1990 and 2007 was just 62 per cent. For now, though, the ratio may not have stopped climbing. According to one forecast, Federal debt as a proportion of GDP is set to exceed 100 per cent between 2012 and 2016.[33]

The last gold bull market only came to an end once the age of uncompensated inflation also came to an end. By 1980, the US had reduced its debt burden to 32 per cent of GDP, down from a peak of 122 per cent in 1946. Having played a central role in resolving the problem of over-indebtedness, inflation itself then became the problem. The Federal Reserve – and central banks elsewhere – therefore hiked interest rates aggressively to choke off these rampant increases in the cost of living.

Not only is excessive debt much the bigger challenge facing the developed world today, but also problematic inflation still seems some way off. In fact, there is not much inflation at all, according to official figures. As of early 2012, Japan continues to suffer with mildly falling consumer prices, while inflation in the US and much of the eurozone also remains largely low and contained. Even if inflation does accelerate as a result of further loose monetary policies, the authorities seem unlikely to intervene decisively to prevent it. Higher real borrowing costs at this stage could render some governments and other big borrowers insolvent.

In light of the outlook for uncompensated inflation, there is surely a good case for gold to go substantially higher than its 2011 peak of $1,925 an ounce in the years ahead. At that price, gold was still somewhat below where it had got to in 1980 in inflation-adjusted terms. Expressed in early 2012 prices, the 1980 peak of $875 would be closer to $2,560. Admittedly, that 1980 peak was totally unsustainable, but that was because of the authorities raising interest rates to unprecedented levels.

HOW TO INVEST IN GOLD

ASSUMING TODAY'S BULL MARKET in gold does indeed continue, we need to consider the best ways to exploit it. It has never been easier to speculate on the price of gold than it is now. As well as buying coins or bullion, there has been a proliferation of financial instruments linked to gold over recent years, including exchange-traded funds (ETFs) and lots of exotic derivative products.

Choosing between these various instruments is mainly a question of determining our precise reason for wanting to own gold. Probably the most popular way of getting exposure to the yellow metal today is via an exchange-traded fund (ETF).

ETFs

On the face of it, an ETF could hardly be more straightforward. The fund buys gold and then lists itself on a stock exchange. The price of the fund goes up and down in line with the price of gold, and investors can deal in shares of the fund as they would an ordinary share, typically paying fairly low annual charges.

Not all gold ETFs are created equal, however. While the assets of some gold ETFs are held in the form of gold itself, others don't own any gold whatsoever. Instead, they simply get exposure to gold-price movements via swap agreements, in which the ETF provider agrees to pay a certain rate to some other party in return for receiving a payment that matches the change in the gold price. This synthetic arrangement usually does a perfectly good job of tracking the gold price and can also be more tax-efficient.

Synthetic ETFs also offer interesting possibilities to speculators who are especially confident that gold is going higher before long. For example, a leveraged ETF goes up and down two or even three times as much as the gold price itself, such that a one per cent move becomes a two or three per cent profit or loss to the ETF's shareholders. Or, for bearish investors, synthetic ETFs also provide an opportunity to profit from falling gold prices, via inverse ETFs, the value of which rises as the gold price declines.

The problem with investing in gold or any other asset in synthetic form comes if the other side in the swap agreement can't keep up its end of the bargain. In that event, the fund provider and its investors merely join a queue of creditors with no guarantee of getting anything back. This risk is much greater during times of market turmoil; precisely the sort of conditions against which we might want to own gold as insurance. So, if we fear meltdown in financial markets, especially involving derivatives, opting for physical gold investments over synthetic versions might be advisable.

Unlike their synthetic brethren, a physical gold ETF will actually be backed with real bullion, which is stored in a vault and is regularly audited. It is even possible to redeem your investment in bars rather than cash, assuming you own a sufficient quantity. This is not enough to satisfy some purists, however, who point out that as the holder of a physical gold ETF, you are merely the owner of a gold-denominated debt security issued by a trust that owns the gold. In other words, there isn't a specific piece of gold with your name on it. For those of this mindset, there are even more direct methods of physical gold ownership available.

DIRECT OWNERSHIP

Traditionally, direct ownership in gold meant keeping coins or bars either at home or in a safety-deposit box. The former has always been a risky option for the simple reason of security; the advantage of having a supply of gold about one's person in case of Armageddon must be balanced against the rather more common hazard of being burgled. Even safety-deposit boxes in banks have also been plundered from time to time by more resourceful thieves.

Investors who wish to own a specific piece of top-quality gold but don't actually require the ability to stroke it every day might consider an online bullion-exchange. This sort of service – of which **BullionVault.com** is the best known – allows investors to buy into bullion that is then stored on their behalf in a high-security vault. The gold in question is allocated to the particular investor, such that he or she is the legal owner of it and can demand delivery of that bar, rather than cash, when the time comes to sell.

An intriguing element of the BullionVault service is that it allows an investor to elect the location of the vault where their particular holding is stored, with a choice of London, New York and Zurich. Gold bugs persistently show a marked preference for Switzerland when it comes to storing gold. Switzerland is widely regarded as more likely to respect property rights, including the right to confidentiality concerning one's ownership.

This is an important point. Governments throughout history have a shabby record of confiscating gold when it has suited them to do so. The most notorious episode was President Roosevelt's Executive Order of 1933 that forbade private ownership of gold coin, bullion or certificates and required citizens to surrender their holdings beyond a token amount to the Federal Reserve.[34] The maximum penalty for defying this seizure was ten years' imprisonment and a $10,000 fine, equivalent to $175,000 in today's money. These restrictions on gold ownership remained largely in place until 1974.

The typical motivation for prohibiting gold ownership is because the yellow metal had become a serious rival to a country's legal tender. In America in the 1930s, people spooked by the collapse of many banks flocked to gold, even though paper money was actually gaining in value as a result of deflation. In recent years in Zimbabwe, the population turned its back on the hyper-inflating Zimbabwe dollar in favour of other countries' currencies and, in certain cases, gold.

Among the more conspiratorially-minded, there is a growing belief that gold could become the target of an official snatch-and-grab operation during a future crisis. In this event, gold stored in certain locations and quoted via stock-market listed vehicles would obviously be more visible and accessible to the authorities than that which was safely concealed in a faraway vault. The main issue for owners of such discreetly held bullion would therefore be whether they were comfortable in disobeying the law of the day.

SHARES IN GOLD-MINING FIRMS

We have already seen how gold has failed miserably to keep up with the stock market over the long run. But might it be possible somehow to get the best of both worlds? Shares in gold-mining companies offer not only exposure to the price of the gold that they extract from the earth, but also to growing cash flows. Mining companies are able to make increasing profits over time, which they can reinvest in their businesses and also pay out as dividends. Gold itself, by contrast, has no cash flow whatsoever, which is the main source of its disadvantage against equities.

Alluring as the idea of having the best of both worlds may be, it doesn't seem to have worked out in practice. Gold mining stocks in the US have lagged behind the price of gold bullion during the current bull market. From the summer of 1999 to the end of 2011, gold went up by 516 per cent, compared to just 224 per cent for the Datastream US Gold Mining Index. Including the effect of reinvested dividends doesn't improve things much either, the total return being 259 per cent.

The longer-term picture for gold mining shares isn't much better. The Barron's Gold Mining Index (BGMI) goes back to 1938. From that year until October 2010, the BGMI rose 2,358 per cent versus a 3,738 per cent gain in the price of gold, as illustrated in Chart 3.3. Looking exclusively at the period from 1968, when the price of gold was liberated from state control, the BGMI gained just 600 per cent compared to the gain of 3,738 per cent for the price of gold (the price of gold was fixed at \$35 in 1933 and remained so all the way up to 1968, so its gain from 1938 to 2010 and 1968 to 2010 is the same).

CHART 3.3 – GOLD AND GOLD MINERS

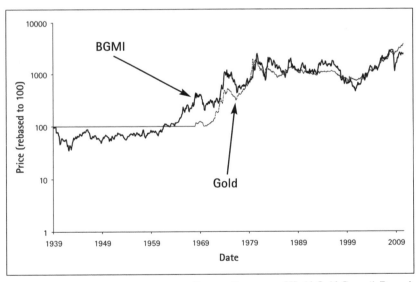

Sources: Datastream, World Gold Council, Barron's

INDIVIDUAL MINING FIRMS

Admittedly, there have been some eye-catching individual success stories among gold mining firms. One of the most prominent examples in recent years has been Randgold Resources, whose operations are based mainly in Mali and whose shares trade on the London Stock Exchange. Since July 2001, its price has risen from £2.37 to a record high of £77.20 in February 2012. Randgold's 33-fold gain compares favourably to bullion's 7-fold gain over the same period; its performance was clearly vastly superior to that of gold itself and of its peers in the mining sector.

While this shows the potential returns available from individual gold-mining equities, the difficulty is how to sort the sheep from the goats. For every Randgold, there are several firms that have failed miserably to keep pace with the price of gold. Unless we have a particular gift for stock-picking, therefore, the safest approach for buying equities in this area is to hold a selection of them.

Perhaps the best argument against using gold mining shares as a substitute for gold itself, though, is diversification. As we saw earlier, one of gold's most desirable properties is its weak – and often negative – relationship with the stock market. This makes it ideal for balancing out the equity risks in our portfolio. By contrast, it is harder to spread equity risk using equities. Gold mining shares in the US have been significantly more positively correlated with the US stock market over time than has gold itself.

Ultimately, there is no single way of owning gold that is necessarily better than all the others. Those who fear financial-market meltdown or government seizure will be more drawn to the most tangible forms of gold investment. Those who do not lie awake at night contemplating such dramatic outcomes may well settle for synthetic alternatives, especially if they desire leveraged returns. But while there is no single method of holding gold that will suit every portfolio, almost every investor should consider holding gold in some form.

ENDNOTES

[28] Datastream: MSWRLD$, BMUS10Y, GOLDBLN.

[29] **www.gold.org/investment/statistics**

[30] 'Zimbabwe Central Bank threatens action on interest rates', Reuters, (31 July 2010).

[31] Philip Aldrick, '1974? Now that was a bear market', *The Daily Telegraph* (27 July 2002).

[32] *Credit Suisse Global Investment Returns Yearbook 2012*, p.57.

[33] Data – historic and forecasted – courtesy of **www.usgovernmentspending.com**

[34] Executive Order 6102, signed by President Franklin D. Roosevelt, 5 April 1933.

CHAPTER 4

BEYOND HYPE: A BALANCED LOOK AT EMERGING MARKETS

IT IS HARD FOR A WESTERNER visiting China not to feel awestruck. Perhaps it is the surprise of seeing vast and previously unheard of cities sprouting up out of the earth. Or, it might be the rather unsettling experience of encountering people who toil dutifully for long hours that would be literally unthinkable back home. Impressions such as these – and many others besides – help explain why China has become such an alluring investment story to outsiders over recent years.

The same is true of many of today's other emerging markets. Nations from Southeast Asia, Latin America and even Africa have undergone a dramatic transformation from a time when they were perceived merely as hot climates, to being hot destinations for equity investment. The likes of India, Brazil and South Africa boast apparent advantages that much of the developed world no longer does, including plentiful and youthful populations, low indebtedness and, at least in certain cases, low taxes and light regulation.

Faith in the power of emerging stock markets has been borne out by investment performance of late. Between January 2000 and January 2012, the MSCI Emerging Markets Index – which includes stocks from 26 poorer nations – rose 87 per cent in US dollar terms.

Some individual emerging stock markets have done even better still. China, for example, gained 112 per cent over the period, and India 153 per cent. By comparison, the MSCI World Index – which only includes stocks from the developed world – *fell* by 16.7 per cent.

An investor's perspective on emerging markets

When approaching emerging markets as an investor, though, it is important not to get carried away. The hype surrounding the prospects for stocks in some of these countries should instead make us cautious. If there is one lesson that we should have learned over the last decade and more, it is about the danger of getting seduced by the latest sensational story. Nor should we blindly invest on the strength of recent performance. One decade's winners can easily become the next decade's losers.

Much of what we hear on the subject of emerging markets comes from those who are promoting investment products in this area. There is also a burgeoning library of books that extol the virtues of buying into developing nations, many of which are the work of those with a significant vested interest. A more promising approach for weighing up emerging markets' prospects is to seek inspiration from some of the excellent academic studies in this field and try to build an investment strategy accordingly.

There are two essential elements to any investment proposition: the return and the risk. There is a natural human tendency to focus on the first of these, and perhaps even to ignore the second altogether. However, if emerging-market equities offer us higher returns this is of course because they come with greater risk attached. As well as considering their returns over time, then, we need to consider here what risks we are running. Specifically, we should examine the danger of getting caught up in another bubble, as well as of other specific emerging-market catastrophes.

Chart 4.1 shows the real growth of the Chinese economy and the returns from Chinese stocks since 1993. Looking at this, it might seem obvious that the high growth of the economy is responsible for the success of the stock market. After all, the two lines have moved closely together. However, the long-term relationship between economic performance and equity returns isn't anything like as straightforward as that. In fact, it is possibly the complete opposite of what intuition suggests that it ought to be.

CHART 4.1 – CHINA'S ECONOMIC AND STOCK MARKET GROWTH

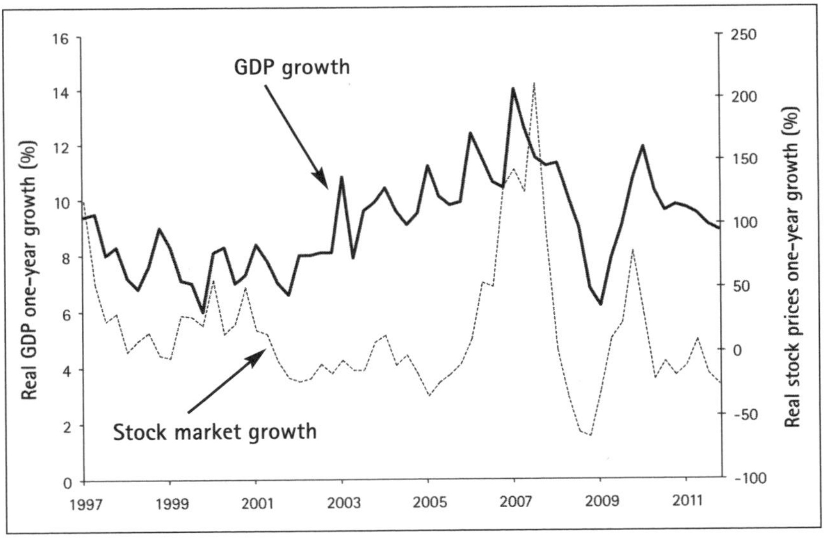

Source: Datastream

THE RELATIONSHIP BETWEEN GROWTH AND RETURNS

In a study covering the entire 20th century, Jay Ritter of the University of Florida found that economic growth and stock-market returns were *negatively* related.[35] For example, Japan enjoyed faster growth in real GDP per capita than any other country covered, but didn't have anything like the best-performing stock market. South Africa and Australia, by contrast, experienced comparatively modest rates of economic growth, but their equity markets were among the biggest winners.

The countries addressed in Professor Ritter's work are, however, largely from the developed world but his findings do seem to apply to emerging markets too. Focusing on the 1970 to 1997 period, Jeremy Siegel of Yale University confirmed the negative relationship for developed markets and GDP growth, but also found that the relationship between stock returns and growth was negligible for 18 emerging markets.[36]

This is certainly not to say that economic growth isn't a good thing in itself, as it clearly produces many benefits. For example, it enables people to lead longer, healthier lives, to have better working conditions and to enjoy more leisure time. The key point, though, is that more economic growth doesn't necessarily end up boosting publicly-traded companies and their profits – others may reap the gains instead.

Despite the conclusions of all this extensive research, superior economic growth prospects typically form an essential part of the story often told to lure investors into buying into emerging markets. And this story is sometimes used to justify investment activity of the wildest sort. Emerging markets have frequently played host to speculative bubbles over time.

Bubble trouble in emerging markets

The most recent such episode was during the 1990s, when vast amounts of foreign capital flooded into Southeast Asian economies such as Thailand, Singapore, Malaysia and Indonesia. Much of this was reflected in huge gains in real estate prices across the region, both in the residential and commercial sectors. Retail premises in Hong Kong more than trebled in value between 1991 and 1997[37], and Singaporean housing quintupled from 1986 to 2010.[38]

Southeast Asian equities also boomed in the 1990s. The Bangkok SET index more than trebled between late 1990 and early 1994, with the Indonesian market recording a similar gain between late 1991 and mid-1997. Naturally, enthusiasts came up with a compelling story and even a catchy name for their darling markets. It was claimed that these *tiger* economies were undergoing an "economic miracle", which therefore justified the sharp gains in the local stock and real-estate markets.

This previous episode of emerging-market fever culminated in the summer of 1997 in what became known as the Asian crisis. The likes of Thailand, the Philippines and Indonesia had become heavily reliant on exports and had also borrowed excessively from abroad. The US dollar – to which they had tied their own currencies – strengthened, making their exports much less attractive. Foreigners began to sell their emerging-market investments, leading to sharp declines in stocks and other Asian assets.

Defining a bubble

To determine whether a bubble has again inflated in emerging markets today – or whether there is a danger of one inflating – we need a more precise idea of what a bubble actually is. It is a term that often gets thrown around carelessly in financial circles, typically to describe any big gain in asset prices that a particular critic happens to disagree with.

The late Charles Kindleberger – one of the greatest ever authorities on financial manias and crashes – defined a bubble as:

> "a sharp rise in the price of an asset or a range of assets in a continuous process, with the initial rise generating expectations of further rises and attracting new buyers – generally speculators interested in profits from trading in the asset rather than its use or earnings capacity."[39]

Kindleberger's definition of a bubble is a good start. We know that the value of any asset is the value today of its future cash flows. So, when investors are buying frantically without any regard for the sort of dividends they can realistically expect, it's a strong clue that a bubble might be inflating. A glance at the chart of a market's price action can tell us quite a bit here. If a stock index is rising in almost vertical fashion, alarm bells ought to start ringing, especially if the price is rising much faster than earnings are or more quickly than dividends can realistically be expected to grow.

Certainly, Southeast Asian stocks experienced very strong gains in the period before 1997. Thai stocks, for example, rose 187 per cent in the three years leading up to their 1994 peak. Chart 4.2 provides an illustration of Thai and Indonesian stock market performance from 1985 to 1998 (rebased to 100 in 1985), with the strong gains up to 1994 visible. However, this doesn't quite compare with some obvious bubble episodes, such as that in hi-tech stocks in the US in the late 1990s or that of silver in 1980. During these episodes, the NASDAQ rocketed 259 per cent, while the semi-precious metal went up 670 per cent.

CHART 4.2 – SOUTHEAST ASIA BOOMING

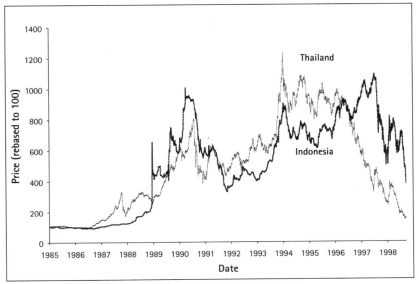

Source: Datastream, indices rebased to 100

While Brazil, Russia, India and China have been catchily labelled as the BRIC countries and are routinely cited in glowing terms, their stock markets have not gone up in anything like the same fashion as US technology stocks or silver when there were bubbles in these areas. Instead, their gains have been altogether steadier, as Chart 4.3 showing the performance of the BRICs from 2007 to 2012, and NASDAQ and silver in their respective bubble periods, illustrates.

CHART 4.3 – BRICs 2007 TO 2012 VERSUS REAL PAST BUBBLES

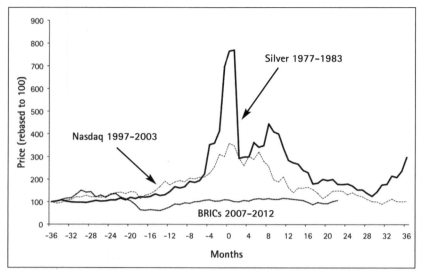

Source: Datastream

A similar picture emerges when we look at valuations for emerging market stocks. In the 1990s, valuations in Asia hurtled upwards. At their respective peaks, the markets of Thailand and Indonesia were valued on price-to-earnings multiples of 31.5 and 33.7, compared to their long-run averages of 15.1 and 18.3.

It is difficult to argue that valuations as of early 2012 are anything like as frothy, however. Table 4.1 shows the price-to-earnings ratios for three of today's most widely followed emerging stock markets, as well as their averages and previous extremes. The Brazilian and Indian markets traded in line with their long-term average PE multiples at the time of writing, while China's market is significantly below its long-run average.

Table 4.1 – Price-to-earnings ratios for Brazil, India and China

	Price-to-earnings (PE) – Feb 2012	Average PE over time	High PE/Low PE
Brazil	12	11.7	21/5
India	18.1	19.2	69/9
China	9.2	19.2	32/4

Source: Datastream

Even considering this evidence that the recent performance of Southeast Asian stocks and the BRICs is not as extreme as certain notable bubbles, we should avoid taking too narrow a view of what a bubble really is. Rampant gains in stock prices and valuations are only one manifestation of bubble-trouble within an economy. As the experience of Southeast Asia in the early 1990s showed, bubbles may take the form of capital-investment sprees and real estate speculation. And when these particular bubbles burst, the fallout tends to drag stocks down too.

Is there a bubble in China?

The most likely bubble in emerging markets today is surely in China. True, that is not immediately obvious in Chinese stock-market price action or valuation. However, there are other telltale signs that a bubble may have inflated in the wider economy. This is particularly true when it comes to lending activity, investment in fixed capital, and real-estate activity.

Cheap credit is an essential element within any bubble. The ability to borrow easily at low rates encourages businesses and investors in financial assets to run risks they otherwise would not. Credit in China has been both cheap and easy-to-come by in recent years. This has been a deliberate policy initiative of the ruling Communist party.

In an effort to get the economy growing faster in 2009 – and thereby head off possible social unrest – the authorities ordered state lenders to swell their loan books by one-third. Chart 4.4 illustrates the expansion of loans by Chinese financial institutions – in billions of yuan – in the period 2002 to 2011.

CHART 4.4 – TOTAL LOANS OF CHINESE FINANCIAL INSTITUTIONS

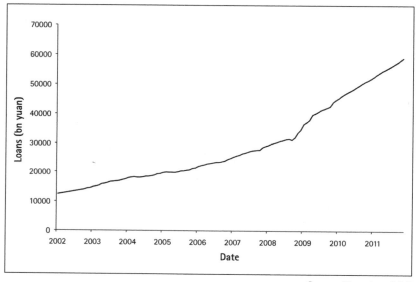

Source: Bloomberg LLP

The ploy did help to accelerate growth very impressively. Having slowed alarmingly from 11.3 per cent in early 2008 to just 6.2 per cent in early 2009, Chinese real GDP growth recovered to more than 11.9 per cent one year later. The economy has continued to expand at more than eight per cent a year ever since. The short-term benefits of this loan-largesse may have come at a very heavy future cost, however.

China had already experienced an unprecedented boom in capital expenditure even before the latest splurge. According to Albert Edwards of Société Générale, a leading French bank, the boom was longer-lasting than any other previous episode, including Japan's spurt in the late 1960s and early 1970s, and the various Southeast

Asia *tiger* economies in the 1990s. It has also been more intense, with capital expenditure equal to more than 50 per cent of the size of the economy at its peak.[40]

The most tangible results of the Chinese bubble are to be found in the vast ghost cities of empty flats dotted around the landscape and also in many redundant shopping malls. What goes for apartment blocks and retail parks applies also to the glut of factories and machinery. When demand for Chinese exports from the US and Europe next contracts, the extent of the oversupply in Chinese manufacturing could become painfully apparent. There are signs this process may be underway in the Chinese property market already.

Many investors seem almost blasé about these risks, however. There seems to be a widespread belief that the Chinese authorities will again prove equal to the task of coping with any economic shock. Anthony Bolton – a legendary UK investor who now runs a China fund for Fidelity – has said one of his reasons for optimism on the country was that its growth trajectory was bolstered by the certainty of central planning, making it a more attractive destination than democracies like India and Indonesia.

Mr Bolton's argument clearly flies in the face of experience. Central planning in economies elsewhere has traditionally led to the massive misallocation of resources, much more so than if markets are left to their own devices. More ominously, though, such faith in China's government to perpetuate the nation's *economic miracle* is typical of the sort of logic that tends to do the rounds during bubbles.

When China's real-estate and capital expenditure bubbles eventually do burst, it will surely have a dramatic impact on the Chinese stock market, even if it is not clearly overvalued at that precise moment. Chinese corporate earnings would likely collapse as would stock prices themselves. In that environment, other emerging equity markets – particularly in Asia – would almost certainly suffer heavy declines too.

Threats to investors taking exposure to emerging markets

Bubbles are dramatic events to which emerging markets may be especially prone, given the exciting growth stories that surround them and their ability to attract flows of hot money from abroad. But getting caught up in the implosion of a bubble is just one danger of buying into these nations. There are also other threats to which investors do not always pay enough attention. These fall into three broad categories: economic, social and political, and malfeasance.

Economic risk

There is a growing belief that today's emerging markets are less risky economically speaking than ever before. This has much to do with indebtedness. The global credit crunch that erupted in 2007 has brought home to many investors just how heavily indebted many of the world's developed economies are. By contrast, many of those emerging economies that are most popular with investors are in much better financial shape, with significantly lower levels of public debt.

According to the International Monetary Fund (IMF), the average gross government debt across developed nations for 2012 was forecast to be 103.7 per cent of GDP. For emerging nations, the average is estimated at a mere 34.6 per cent. This gap is forecast to widen further, with average indebtedness in the advanced world to hit 107.3 per cent by 2016 and the emerging world's average expected to shrink to 30.2 per cent. In 2006, the year before the credit crunch struck, the figures were 74.1 per cent and 36.6 per cent respectively.[41]

The situation as it plays out may be even worse than these figures suggest. Most advanced economies are committed to providing expensive pension and healthcare programs to their rapidly ageing populations over the coming decades. Were these implicit liabilities reflected on governments' balance sheets, the indebtedness of the US, UK, Japan and many other nations would balloon to several hundred per cent of GDP. Emerging economies, on the other hand, have much lighter welfare and pension provision and much younger populations on the whole.

The lighter indebtedness of the emerging world may be a legitimate part of the case in favour of investing in their economies over the coming years, but we need to add some perspective here by reminding ourselves of some of their ongoing drawbacks. For a start, inflation has traditionally been much higher in emerging economies than in developed economies and this remains the case right up to the present, as Table 4.2 shows.

Table 4.2 – Comparing inflation in emerging and developed economies

	Average inflation 2000-2010 (%)	Average inflation 2010-2012 (%)
China	1.9	4.3
Brazil	6.9	5.8
India	5.6	10.4
Indonesia	8.4	5.1
Russia	13.9	7.6
Vietnam	6.7	12.4
UK	1.9	3.9
US	2.6	2.4
Eurozone	2.2	2.5
Switzerland	0.9	0.4
Japan	-0.3	-0.5

Source: Datastream, IMF

High inflation can be extremely toxic to the economy. Above all, it creates uncertainty. When prices in the wider economy get out of control, it makes it harder for most businesses to plan investment projects and to conduct their everyday operations. Consumers – particularly the poorest – suffer declining standards of living as their incomes fail to keep up with price rises. Eventually, the authorities are forced to take action to restrain the inflation, the side-effect of which is typically to strangle economic growth, perhaps even causing recession.

The uncertainty caused by high inflation can easily hurt stock returns. First of all, it tends to increase volatility in the stock market, which can make equities less appealing to investors. Secondly, rising inflation is typically reflected in falling share-price valuations. Specifically, the price-to-earnings ratio that investors are willing to pay comes down as consumer prices rise, reflecting the greater risk of investing in equities.

In some circumstances, high inflation in emerging economies can develop into hyperinflation. The International Accounting Standards Board defines hyperinflation as when the rate of inflation approaches a rate where prices double every three years, equivalent to about 26 per cent annually. Hyperinflation is typically a nightmare for stockholders. In Brazil, the annual rate of inflation ballooned to 6,821 per cent in January 1990. At the same time, the country's Bovespa equity index was up by only 1,237 per cent on the previous year – meaning that stocks were seeing their real value destroyed.

Inflation could easily become more of a problem in emerging markets in the coming years – and perhaps not for reasons of those countries' own making. The indebted nations of the developed world are already in the process of trying to inflate away their massive liabilities with artificially low interest rates and by engaging in quantitative easing – or printing money – as discussed in Chapter 2. These easy-money policies have unleashed heavy speculation in commodities in recent years. The CRB index – which covers a broad range of commodities including foodstuffs, fuel and metals – rose 86 per cent between March 2009 and February 2012.

Quantitative easing in America also tends to force down the value of the US dollar. To stop their own currencies from getting too strong against the dollar and thereby keep their exports competitive, emerging nations often respond to easier money in the US by printing money themselves. When China in particular expands its money-stock in this way, commodity prices – and inflation in China – have been shown to rise too. With such policies likely to continue in the US and other developed markets, more aggressive inflation is a real risk in emerging markets.

Social and political risk

Inflation isn't just an economic risk for emerging markets; it can also have important social and political consequences. Whereas in developed markets, rising prices crimp consumers' ability to buy discretionary items, in poorer nations they can leave people without sufficient food. Widespread hunger can easily spill over into popular unrest. Algeria and Tunisia suffered major rioting in early 2011, resulting partly from the spiralling cost of food. The Tunisian uprising culminated in the overthrow of the country's dictatorship and the installation of a new, democratic government.

Although the Tunisian revolution ended happily from the perspective of human rights, it hit the emerging nation's stock market hard. The Tunisian exchange dropped 27 per cent from its highs of October 2010 to its lows of February 2011. Despite the country's subsequent transition to democracy, Tunisian equities had only recovered just over half of their losses by early March 2012.

The progression from discontent over food costs to demands for greater freedom will not have gone unnoticed in China. The authorities of the world's largest emerging market know that their grip on power depends very much on their ability to ensure that peasants continue to get new jobs in factories, that factory-workers keep getting higher wages and that the middle class continues to enrich itself. Even if the government manages to pull off this trick, the people are ultimately likely to demand political freedom to accompany their economic liberty.

It could be that China enjoys a gentle and gradual journey to political freedom over the coming years. Even if the process is bloodless, the resulting uncertainty can be damaging to both the economy and investments. Taking Russia as an example, once released from the shackles of Communist rule in 1991, it underwent several years of economic decline, increased lawlessness and the disintegration of its territories. Some of the effects of this still trouble the country today, especially when it comes to the rule of law.

MALFEASANCE RISK

Russia is often mentioned as one of the most exciting emerging markets of recent years, typically in the same breath as Brazil, India and China. While this is not unjustified, the country also provides some unfortunate examples of emerging-market malfeasance as the rule of law is not yet as strong as it could be. The Russian legal system is still in the process of catching up with that of the rest of the capitalist world, and there have been some prominent cases were it has not upheld the property rights of businesses and individuals in the way that it ideally should have done.

Corporate governance – how companies are run and the relationships between their managers, shareholders and others – is also perceived as underdeveloped in Russia. Admittedly, the country has made progress towards establishing appropriate rules and conventions in recent years. However, it is often said the rules are not always well enforced and sometimes contradict each other. Also, sanctions for significant violations of the law remain too light.

UNRELIABLE ECONOMIC DATA

The precise costs of inadequate corporate governance and legal shortcomings more generally are, of course, hard to quantify for emerging markets. One obvious way in which they may be reflected is in lower stock-market valuations. However, stock market valuations themselves can be rather opaque in these countries – along with the true macroeconomic situation. Data relating to these matters are essential for making well-grounded investment decisions, but that data which is available is not always reliable.

At the macroeconomic level, the authorities in several key emerging markets have a habit of painting performance in the most flattering light – or at least brushing over the most inconvenient patches. A curious discrepancy arose in China in 2009 where the government's published figures showed the nation's industrial value-added (IVA) output growth was expanding at a healthy clip, but electricity consumption – which had traditionally moved in line with IVA – was declining.[42]

It was widely suspected at the time that the Chinese government had rigged its estimates in order to bolster its reputation for economic management at a time of weakness in the international economy. China also raised eyebrows around the world at the height of the Asian crisis in 1997, when it declared only slightly reduced GDP of 7.8 per cent growth. One independent estimate put the true rate at minus 0.1 per cent.[43] In a leaked diplomatic cable, the Chinese Vice Premier Li Keqiang had smilingly admitted to US Ambassador Clark T. Randt in 2007 that Chinese GDP figures were "man-made" and "for reference only."[44]

It is not only totalitarian states that cook the books in this fashion. Argentina – an emerging market and a democracy – has routinely produced inflation data that absurdly understates the country's runaway price increases. Independent statisticians within Argentina who have dared to contradict this misrepresentation have faced harassment from the authorities, including demands for cripplingly large fines and having criminal complaints filed against them.[45] In February 2012, *The Economist* magazine ceased to publish the official data, substituting it with estimates produced by private consultants based beyond the regime's clutches.[46]

POOR QUALITY FINANCIAL STATEMENTS

Even more difficult than obtaining realistic estimates of emerging nations' growth or inflation may be getting a true picture of the health of their publicly-traded companies. Financial statements from listed firms in these nations are not necessarily of a comparable standard to those in developed markets. In China, for example, the practice of shuffling revenues and costs between reporting periods in order to avoid showing consecutive losses is believed to be prevalent.[47]

In conditions where accounting standards are not up to scratch, the really useful information about companies is often restricted to privileged insiders. China's stock market is seen by many Chinese retail investors as being riddled with corruption, principally involving fund managers exploiting tip-offs for their own private accounts.[48] While *rat-trading* – as insider trading is known in China – is a criminal offence, proper monitoring and enforcement have been lacking in recent years, according to the Corporate Governance Think Thank at China Europe International Business School.[49]

Recognising the numerous pitfalls of investing in emerging markets is not the same as saying that they are to be avoided altogether. The experience of the decade since 2000 demonstrates clearly the benefits that are to be had from buying into equities from these less mature countries. Investors simply need to be constantly aware of the sort of dangers that we have explored so far and to construct portfolios with these factors in mind.

Using emerging markets for diversification

It is essential that we think in terms of entire portfolios rather than of individual holdings within them because a key reason for investing in emerging markets as well as in developed markets is to balance out risks. That means understanding how shares from each category move together over time.

Chart 4.5 shows the correlation between the MSCI Emerging Markets Index and developed-world equities, in the form of the MSCI World Index.

CHART 4.5 – CORRELATION BETWEEN DEVELOPED MARKET AND EMERGING MARKET EQUITIES

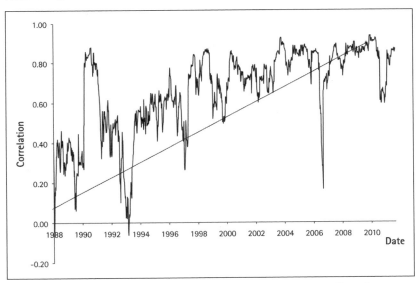

Source: MSCI, via Datastream

In the late 1980s and early 1990s, the correlation between emerging and developed markets was generally low and occasionally negative. Since then, however, it has been much more consistently and strongly positive.

The reason for this increasingly close relationship is most probably globalisation. In the 1970s, individual emerging market economies were rather more insulated, while capital was restricted from flowing in and out. Now, though, emerging economies do more business with the rest of the world, while barriers to investment have been swept away over recent decades. Capital flows effortlessly around the world, with similar investment strategies applied simultaneously by investors across different markets.

These stronger relationships between developed and emerging markets make it harder for us to lay off our risks, especially during periods of weakness when we most need to be able to do so.

PICKING AN EMERGING MARKETS INVESTMENT

The next step is to determine which individual markets are most attractive. Thanks to recent academic research, we know that economic growth is not the key to predicting stock returns. So, what is a good reason for investing in a particular country's stock market?

MARKET VALUATIONS

Jay Ritter suggests that we should look at valuations, specifically the price-to-earnings ratio, or its inverse, the earnings-to-price ratio, known as the *earnings yield*. Rather than taking a single year's earnings, he favours using the average earnings of the last ten years, an approach which smoothes out fluctuations caused by the business cycle. The idea is to buy when this cyclically-adjusted PE ratio is low.

Chart 4.6 demonstrates this approach in practice. The solid line shows the cyclically-adjusted PE valuation for Thailand's Bangkok SET index, aligned with the subsequent three-year performance that would have been achieved from buying at point. For example, the very low cyclically-adjusted PE of 4.2 in 1998 was followed by a 56 per cent return over the next three years. By contrast, the very high cyclical-adjusted PE of 55 in 1990 gave way to a 16.8 per cent loss over the next three years.

CHART 4.6 – BANGKOK SET VALUATION AND RETURNS

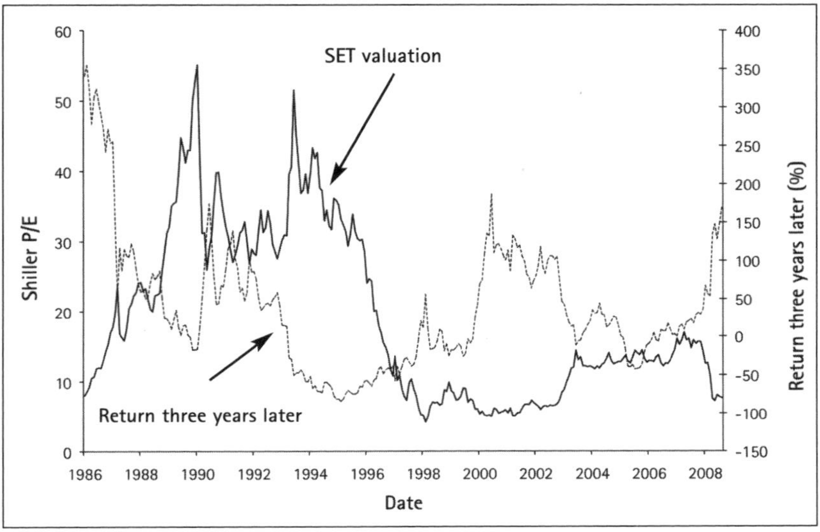

Source: Datastream

As well as looking at emerging markets' valuations on their own, we should also compare them to developed markets' valuations. Once again, the logic is straightforward. Emerging markets are more likely to be a desirable investment when they are cheaply valued in relation to their developed world counterparts. An effective technique here is simply to express the current year's valuation on the MSCI Emerging Markets index as a proportion of the valuation of the MSCI World index.

This approach worked particularly well in 2001, when it correctly predicted that emerging markets would beat developed market stocks over the coming year. In 2007, its message was the exact opposite, but once again proved entirely correct, as emerging markets underperformed during the international financial meltdown of 2008.

EMERGING VALUE OR EMERGING GROWTH?

It also pays to think closely about the style of the emerging market shares we hold. For the developed world, there is a wealth of studies that show that value (or *cheap*) stocks have soundly beaten growth (or *expensive*) shares over time. The same consideration seems to apply to emerging nations too. The MSCI Emerging Markets Value Index has outperformed the MSCI Emerging Markets Growth Index by 2.6 per cent a year between 2000 and 2012.

Within the last decade and more, there have admittedly been shorter periods where growth stocks have got the better of value stocks in the emerging world. These have tended to be the times when the outlook for the developed world's economy has seemed most promising, as measured by leading indicators of economic activity. One reason for this may be that better economic prospects in the developed world tend to engender greater optimism generally, encouraging investors to seek out riskier, growth-orientated equities.

Of course, there is no reason why the coming decade will necessarily resemble the most recent one. This applies not only to investment styles within emerging markets, but to emerging markets as a whole. Whereas in 2002, emerging stocks were cheap versus developed-world stocks, they are neither particularly cheap nor dear as of early 2012.

What experience does teach us is that emerging market stocks should become more cheaply valued at some point in the coming years – and investments in these hot markets are best made when their valuations go a bit cold.

Endnotes

[35] Jay R. Ritter, '*Economic growth and equity returns*', University of Florida.

[36] Jeremy Siegel, *Stocks for the Long Run* (McGraw Hill Professional, 2nd edition, 1998).

[37] Charles Collyns and Abdellhak Senhadji, '*Lending booms, Real Estate Bubbles and the Asian Crisis*', IMF Working Paper/02/20 (January 2002).

[38] www.singaporerealestate.info

[39] J. Eatwell, *The New Palgrave Dictionary of Economics* (Palgrave MacMillan, 1987), p.281.

[40] Albert Edwards, SG Cross Asset Research, 'Global Strategy Weekly', *Société Générale* (20 October 2011), p. 3.

[41] IMF Fiscal Monitor (April 2011), p. 127.

[42] Krugman, New York Times Blogs, krugman.blogs.nytimes.com/2009/05/29/what-you-dont-know

[43] New York Society of Security Analysts, post.nyssa.org/nyssa-news/2011/07/understanding-chinas-economic-indicators.html

[44] wikileaks.org/cable/2007/03/07BEIJING1760.html#

[45] Fight over Argentina's inflation rate pits government against private economists.

[46] 'Don't lie to me, Argentina', *The Economist* (25 February 2012).

[47] 'Towards Mature Corporate Governance Standards in China', *Forbes India* (2 December 2011).

[48] 'Insider trading is a major issue', *Shanghai Daily* (3 March 2012).

[49] *Forbes India* (2 December 2011).

CHAPTER 5

DREAD, DENIAL AND DEFAULT

THE SENSE OF DREAD BEFOREHAND is often worse than the deed itself. That was certainly true in the case of Greece defaulting on its debts. The prospect of Greece failing to meet its obligations spooked financial markets repeatedly from 2010 onwards. However, once it was actually confirmed in March 2012 that the country would not repay its creditors in full, the markets barely reacted at all. Even so, while the ultimate response may have been gentle, this is not to say that sovereign debt defaults are in any way painless.

There was nothing novel about Greece's default. Sovereign nations have done exactly the same on repeated occasions throughout history. Particularly in recent years, however, these defaults have tended to take place in poor countries, rather than in economically developed states. They have also typically occurred in clusters. Crises of debt very often have causes that are common to several states simultaneously. The Greek default may thus turn out not to be an isolated event.

Despite Greece's rude reminder that default is a risk that exists fairly close to home, we are still not prepared for the consequences of a potential new era of sovereign debt defaults. To address this shortcoming, we need a better understanding of how these events come about and what impacts they have, both in the defaulting country itself and elsewhere. Three sovereign defaults or near-defaults from recent decades – those in Mexico, Russia and Argentina – provide some very useful lessons in this regard.

THE MEXICAN PESO CRISIS OF 1994

TEQUILA HAS BEEN BLAMED for countless nasty hangovers. Appropriately, therefore, Mexico's 1994 debt-shock has become known as the *tequila crisis* in a nod to the country's potent national drink. While certain elements of the turmoil – including a revolt by Mayan Indians – may seem to mark the tequila episode out as typical of a crisis in some exotic land, the underlying ingredients are very familiar.

PRECEDING ECONOMIC REFORMS

In the years preceding the crisis, Mexico had actually undergone numerous economically beneficial reforms. Having come to power in a rather dubious election in 1988, Carlos Salinas reversed much of the country's revolutionary socialist legacy. He took on Mexico's powerful trade union movement in an effort to liberalise labour laws and freed peasants to sell their smallholdings of land. Within four years, all but 15 per cent of state-owned enterprises had been privatised. Inflation fell from 180 per cent a year in early 1988 to just seven per cent by 1994. Mexico was also heading for free trade with the US and Canada, under the North American Free Trade Agreement, which was due to come into force in early 1995.

Not all of the reforms were well thought out, however.[50] The elimination of statutory capital-reserve requirements for banks was an invitation to trouble, especially since the government made it known that it stood behind the banks. In response, the banks relaxed their lending criteria and expanded their loan books dramatically.

In the words of Francisco Gil-Diaz, a former Vice Governor of the Bank of Mexico, the effect was to create a credit boom "of such magnitude and speed that it overwhelmed weak supervisors, the scant capital of some banks, and even borrowers." Direct credit for consumer durables, for example, expanded at a rate of one-quarter every year during this period.

Other reforms, while necessary, were handled insensitively. Salinas' agricultural reforms sparked a revolt among Mayan Indians in Chiapas, Mexico's southernmost province, on New Year's Day 1994. The uprising lasted only two weeks, after which the government entered talks with the rebels. The air of instability persisted, however, thanks to a long-running media campaign by the rebel leader Subcomandante Marcos, which aimed to expose the country's endemic corruption problems. This spooked international investors throughout 1994.

SPECULATORS ATTACK THE PESO

It was during this period of nervousness that the Mexican peso came repeatedly under attack by speculators. The country ran a managed exchange-rate policy, under which the peso was linked to the US dollar and prevented from moving out of a certain range. To maintain this policy, the Bank of Mexico had to be vigilant and constantly intervene in the markets when the peso became either too strong or too weak. To combat the speculative attacks of 1994, the bank was forced to use its reserves of other currencies to buy pesos. Its defence efforts sapped its reserves, drastically reducing its ability to pursue its day-to-day exchange-rate policies.

Mexico had also borrowed substantially from foreigners in other currencies. It owed US$29 billion in the form of *tesobonos*, or dollar-indexed government securities, while it also had to make short-term repayments of US$57.9 billion, according to a Bank for International Settlements (BIS) paper[51] by José Julián Sidaoui,

Deputy Governor of the Bank of Mexico. Following the speculative attacks, Mexico lacked sufficient foreign currency reserves to meet these various overseas obligations.

The dollar-indexation of the *tesobonos* meant that they offered holders protection against depreciation of the peso. Upon maturity, the deal was that the Mexican government had to pay the holder of a *tesobono* however many pesos were required to buy a fixed quantity of US dollars, with the sum being computed, as Sidaoui explains, "by applying the spot exchange rate prevailing in the market two days in advance of maturity."

Maintaining the peso within its set range against the US dollar demanded high interest rates. The big gap between Mexican and US rates saw huge amounts of capital flow into the country. Mexican corporations found it easy to raise money from overseas, despite the poor credit rating that both they and their government enjoyed. Foreigners were happy to earn a generous yield on their Mexican holdings, while Mexican consumers enjoyed cheaper imports. One consequence of this was that Mexico's current account deficit doubled to $15 billion by 1991 and almost doubled again by late 1994.

The gap between Mexican and US interest rates narrowed significantly in 1994. The US Federal Reserve raised rates, doubling them in the 12 months to February 1995. Foreign investors therefore wanted even higher rates in order to hold Mexican investments and began dumping older government bonds that did not have dollar indexation. Foreign holdings of *tesobonos* swelled from $5 billion at the start of 1994 to tens of billions by December.[52] Above all, the debts were due for repayment within an uncomfortably short timeframe, on average just ten months into the future.

Devaluation triggers the crisis

Despite the clear stresses and strains within Mexico's economy, the trigger for the crisis of the peso still came as a surprise. On 18 December 1994, new President Ernesto Zedillo met with some of the country's wealthiest business folk. While the ostensible topic of conversation was a planned crackdown on rebels in the Chiapas province, it was widely suspected that the new leader may have tipped off the assembled magnates about a potential devaluation of the nation's currency. The next day, rich Mexicans were seen to convert large sums of pesos into billions of US dollars.[53] On 20 December, the Mexican government announced a 13 per cent devaluation of the peso.

Foreign investors subsequently fled Mexico – and also other countries in the region – even more rapidly than they had embraced them. Within months, the peso had halved in value against the dollar. In order to repay its bondholders their dues, the country was forced to go cap in hand for assistance from both the US and the International Monetary Fund (IMF). The latter provided Mexico with a US$50 billion bailout in order to help it avoid a default. The Mexican economy shrank painfully by more than six per cent in 1995.[54] Unemployment rose sharply, while real wages shrank significantly. The percentage of the population classified as living in extreme poverty almost doubled to around 40 per cent.[55]

Swift response, quick recovery

The tough fiscal discipline that the IMF demanded from Mexico in return for the bailout paid off. Mexico's economy recovered fairly strongly from its mid-1990s malaise. Whereas real GDP shrank at a 7.9 per cent annualised rate at its nadir in the second quarter of 1995, it had recovered to a positive rate of 6.4 per cent just one year later.[56] It continued to grow impressively thereafter into late 2000. Despite a sharp recession during the global financial crisis in 2009, the country's 21st century performance has also been impressive.

Unlike in the case of Greece today, both Mexico and the outside world reacted swiftly and decisively to solve the crisis. "While Europe took years to make decisions, we made decisions with the US and the International Monetary Fund in two months," said Luis Tellez, who was at the time Chief of Staff to President Ernesto Zedillo.[57] Public spending in 1995 was slashed by ten per cent in real terms, value added tax was raised from 10 to 15 per cent, while the government pledged to run a balanced budget during 1995.[58] Government deficits in Mexico are nowadays capped by law.

Admittedly, Mexico's reforms took place in rather more conducive circumstances than those in which the likes of Greece find themselves today. The outside world – and especially Mexico's major trading partner, the US – was enjoying healthy economic growth at that time. As a result, exports played a big part in restoring its fortunes after 1995. Mexico also had its own currency, which meant that much of the necessary adjustments occurred via exchange-rate devaluation, rather than only by way of wage cuts and other austerity measures. By contrast, Greece and its troubled European peers are trying to implement painful reforms against a backdrop of weak growth in their export markets and whilst locked into the still-overvalued euro.

THE RUSSIAN DEFAULT OF 1998

THE YEARS AFTER THE COLLAPSE of the Soviet Union were harsh for Russia. The country suffered lawlessness, economic decline and major losses of territory and international standing. Its international humiliation was completed in 1998 when it defaulted on its debts. Russia's political culture played a major role in bringing about this default. Specifically, practices from the old Soviet Union lingered on into the new era, with disastrous effects.

Soviet era practices linger on

According to Yegor Gaidar, who had served as Prime Minister of Russia in 1992, the country's bureaucracy and industry was accustomed to *soft budgeting*, basically a lack of strict financial accountability. This can be sustainable in a socialist system, as the state's absolute control over hiring and firing managers keeps those managers focused on their enterprise's objectives. Therefore, hard administrative controls had offset soft budgeting in the days of the Soviet Union. However, while the former died along with the USSR, the latter persisted. The result was a lack of direction, inefficiency and waste, along with a great deal of corruption.[59]

Other hangovers from the Soviet period were the practice of delaying or writing off taxes and providing loans on sweetheart terms so long as the enterprise met objectives set by the state. "This combination of feeble budgetary controls, weak administrative controls and *old boy* cronyism engendered an inefficient, stagnant and extremely corrupt environment," wrote Mr Gaidar.

Falling taxes and rising inflation

One urgent need was for the Russian state to get serious about tax collection, instead of putting up with shrinking tax receipts as business after business cheated the tax system. "In Central European countries, such as Hungary and Poland, that found themselves in a similar situation, and where these aspirations [to conform to Western norms of macroeconomic stabilisation] were reinforced by the elite's commitment to join the European Union, governments acted resolutely and quickly to impose serious, not to say, harsh, financial discipline on enterprises," wrote Mr Gaidar.[60]

Unfortunately, Russia did not follow these prescriptions. With little cash in the economy and stunted tax revenues, the Russian government was forced to look overseas to meet its borrowing requirements and ran up big debts to outsiders. Internally, the problem of tax collection became "a political struggle about what constituted the essence of the emerging economic system, whether it was to be a system in which the relationship between the state and enterprises was to be regulated by law, or whether it would be business as usual, based on political influence and personal contacts."[61] As this struggle played out, Russia muddled along, racking up persistent annual budget deficits of around six to seven per cent.

The combined effect of falling tax receipts and rising inflation seriously undermined the Russian state's ability to borrow in the domestic market. President Boris Yeltsin's hapless administration seemed unable to implement the drastic cuts in expenditure that would be necessary to bring the deficit under control. Yeltsin had peremptorily fired his entire government in March 1998, sacking Prime Minister Viktor Chernomyrdin and the entire cabinet, on the grounds that insufficient efforts were being made to solve the country's economic problems.

It was not all bad, however. The government had a year earlier successfully rescheduled loans contracted by the former Soviet regime. The agreement was seen as a major step to restoring international confidence in Russia, which after all had massive oil reserves and a substantial capacity to generate export revenues. Inflation was reduced from 131 per cent in 1995 to 22 per cent in 1996 and thereafter to 11 per cent by 1997.

OVERESTIMATION OF CREDITWORTHINESS

Russia was nevertheless regarded as more creditworthy than it really should have been at this time. According to a study by Abbigail Chiodo and Michael Owyan of the St. Louis Federal Reserve[62], Russia's credit status was largely a result of the recognition accorded to the country by the Paris Club, a multinational body concerned with international debts. Around a quarter of Russia's assets were in the form of essentially unrecoverable debts owed to the former

Soviet Union by impoverished allies like Cuba, Mongolia and Vietnam. The Paris Club used inappropriate exchange rates in its calculations, based on the old official Soviet rate of 0.6 roubles to the dollar, rather than the true one of 5 to 6 roubles.[63] This unjustified perception of creditworthiness enabled Russian banks to expand their foreign borrowing from seven per cent of assets in 1994 to 17 per cent in 1997.

Russia's situation in this regard was analogous to that of the peripheral countries of the eurozone. The likes of Greece, Spain and Portugal were able to amass substantial obligations at very low interest rates thanks to their membership of the euro. Whereas in the past these nations were required to pay significantly more to borrow than Germany, they were ultimately able to borrow at very similar rates, despite their generally much weaker economic and financial positions. There may also have been an implicit belief in the cases of both Russia and the European peripheral states that the entities involved were too big to be allowed to fail.

By 1998, Russia needed to achieve annual economic growth of two per cent to enable it to meet interest payments on its existing borrowings. Instead, its economy contracted by 4.9 per cent that year, partly as a result of the Asian financial crisis, which had begun in the summer of 1997. Asian currencies slumped and speculators soon began to turn their attention to the rouble. Deciding that it too was vulnerable, the speculators attacked. Russia's central bank weathered the storm, but drained its currency reserves by $6 billion in so doing. The price of oil fell in the wake of the Asian crisis, as did that of other commodities, which crimped Russia's vital export earnings.

INVESTORS BAIL OUT

Investors began to fret over a potential devaluation of the rouble by the Russia's Central Bank. Institutions bailed out of both Russian shares and sovereign debt. Oil was down to $11 a barrel, half its price a year earlier. Despite a comparatively modest rate of inflation of ten per cent, the Central Bank was forced to offer a ruinous rate of 150 per cent on short-term government bonds in order to try and refinance its debts that were becoming due. Corporations were also facing a massive borrowing squeeze, with some $3 billion in loans due for refinancing in September 1998.

In desperation, the Russian government turned to the IMF. The rescue package proposed by the IMF in July amounted to additional assistance of some $11.2 billion. Of this, $4.8 billion was due to be disbursed immediately, but this was still insufficient to ward off the subsequent default.

As the summer drew on, Russian financial markets descended into chaos. By August 1998, the stock market had shed more than three-quarters of its value from the start of the year, while the yield on rouble-denominated bonds had surged to more than 200 per cent. The government bowed to the inevitable, devaluing the rouble, defaulting on its domestic debt and ceasing payments on rouble-denominated debts. Russian commercial banks were given a three-month period of grace in respect of their obligations to foreign creditors.[64] The Russian default was now a fact.

DEFAULT AND THEREAFTER

Default and devaluation were humbling for Russia, but they did the trick. After a very painful six months, the Russian economy began to boom once more. A recovery in the price of commodities – and particularly of crude oil – ushered in considerable prosperity. In the first eight years of the new millennium, the economy grew by some 70 per cent, while industrial production expanded by three-quarters.[65] Buoyed by rising oil revenues, the Russian government under President Vladimir Putin was able to repay significant amounts of its debt.

Russia's dire situation in the late 1990s had several parallels with Greece's today. The country had linked its currency to the US dollar, which had similar effects to Greece locking itself into the euro. Each country subsequently enjoyed lower borrowing costs and inflation, but suffered from an increasing lack of competitiveness as investors began to get nervous and borrowing costs rose to unsustainable levels. Unlike Greece, however, Russia had greater control of its own destiny. Although a difficult decision to take, it was able to devalue its currency.

At the time, Russia faced dark threats that were it to default it would find itself shut out of international credit markets for years to come, while foreigners would be unwilling to invest directly or indirectly in the country. Instead, Russia became one of the hottest destinations for emerging market investors in the early 21st century, frequently mentioned in the same breath as Brazil, India and China. Admittedly, another key difference between Russia and today's European problem-cases is that Russia had plentiful natural resources, prices of which boomed for many years consecutively.

THE ARGENTINIAN DEFAULT OF 2001 TO 2002

SEEDS OF THE DEFAULT

THE SEEDS OF ARGENTINA'S 2001 default were sown around two decades earlier. The military dictatorship that gave up power in 1983 left behind an 18 per cent unemployment rate and its industry in an enfeebled state. The democratic government that replaced the junta borrowed heavily to finance the introduction of a new currency, the austral. From the outset, the austral was beset by inflation running at in excess of ten per cent a month. By July 1989, inflation hit 200 per cent per month and topped 5,000 per cent for the year. Wages did not keep abreast of the price rise, with the real wage falling by 50 per cent.

The economic turmoil triggered serious social unrest. Following a spate of riots, the government of President Raúl Alfonsín resigned, giving way to the administration of Carlos Menem. The new President had ambitious plans for economic reform, but saw hyperinflation as a major obstacle to their implementation. Menem appointed Domingo Cavallo to head the Ministry of Economy and Cavallo called in the IMF. Together, Cavallo and the IMF drafted the Convertibility Plan, which pegged the new Argentinean peso to the US dollar at a one-to-one exchange rate.[66] The rampant money printing stopped and certain benefits were soon felt.

After years of runaway price growth, inflation came down to just 0.1 per cent in 1996. The following year, the Argentinean economy expanded at an impressive six per cent clip. All was not entirely well, however, as Argentina was rolling over large amounts of sovereign debt, creating new loans and taking on further debt. While the peso's link to the US dollar maintained confidence in the currency at home and abroad, it had the unintended effect of suddenly introducing vast amounts of cheap credit into the economy. Where citizens had previously needed wheelbarrows full of money to buy foreign goods, they could now buy them on favourable, dollar-based terms.

As a result of this, imports came flooding into Argentina while dollars gushed outwards. The cheap imported goods devastated many local industries, intensifying the country's unemployment problem. Menem's reform program, widely hailed as a success from 1991 to 1994, began to run into the sand. At the same time, the IMF continued to provide financial support to Argentina on the understanding that the government would pursue further reforms, but which were either not implemented or only partly implemented.

Banking scandal and removal of the US dollar peg

The beginning of the end came in the form of a banking scandal. Elisa Carrio and Gustavo Gutiérrez, two Argentine parliamentarians, alleged that the country's banking system was complicit in massive corruption and criminality. They singled out Pedro Pou – the governor of Argentina's Central Bank – for covering up money-laundering activities. Pou was a staunch advocate of the peso's link to the US dollar, which was by now widely seen as a straitjacket that was inhibiting the economy. Adherence to this policy made it impossible to improve its competitive position by devaluation.

By law, Argentina's Central Bank could only introduce fresh pesos against new foreign exchange reserves, but its currency reserves were already hugely depleted as a result of paying for imports. Argentina therefore found itself with very tight monetary policy at a time when its economy was contracting sharply. The ire of the country's industrialists and much of the population was focused on the unfortunate governor of the Central Bank. Mr Pou was ignominiously relieved of his duties in April 2001, charged with "bad conduct."[67] He was replaced by Domingo Cavallo, formerly President Menem's finance director.

To ease Argentina's situation, Cavallo switched the peso's peg from the US dollar to a selection of currencies. This plan had worked in certain other situations elsewhere, but it did not do so on this occasion. The timing of the move was perhaps the main problem. Financial markets interpreted the suggestion of a change to the peg to mean there was a staged devaluation of the peso in the offing, which would hurt foreign holders of Argentine bonds. As investors took flight, Argentina's government borrowing costs soared.

THE CRISIS BUILDS

On the advice of the IMF, Argentina's government had tried to reduce its debt burden, which was at that time equal to 50 per cent of the size of the country's economy. Within its first week in office, the new administration carried out spending cuts worth about US$1.4 billion. Further cuts and tax increases followed soon thereafter. Economic growth dried up almost completely.

Having been able to borrow at a rate of nine per cent in July 2000, Argentina found itself required to pay 16 per cent when it tried to sell bonds again four months later.

In desperation, Argentina turned from the bond markets to the IMF, the World Bank and the US Treasury, all of which demanded the country impose a seventh round of austerity measures. As part of these cutbacks, leading civil servants were paid in IOUs, as no cash was available. An angry rash of strikes ensued. By December 2001, the unemployment rate stood at 20 per cent. The IMF refused to release US$1.3bn in loans, citing the country's inability to make the necessary further budget cuts.

Argentinean financial assets were lain waste. The MerVal stock index dropped by more than seven per cent overnight, while the yield on Argentinean government bonds soared to 42 per cent above those on US Treasuries.[68] The sense of panic was not confined to foreign investors, though. Seeing the writing on the wall, Argentinean consumers rushed to withdraw their money, triggering a run on the banks. The government responded by freezing all bank accounts and then placing strict limits on withdrawal amounts. With the economy effectively starved of cash, violent street protests erupted in the week before Christmas 2001.

The BBC's commentary on events in Argentina at that time is particularly noteworthy, as it emphasises the suddenness with which the end can come, however leisurely the build-up has been:

"Argentina's desperate economic crisis has been long in the making, but the violence and the serious political ramifications it provoked came suddenly. During the day on Wednesday, the country saw some of the worst rioting in a decade as the government's austerity measures continued to bite. Police fired tear gas and rubber bullets to disperse looters near the capital, Buenos Aires, as people prised open shops and carted away everything they could. Unrest also spread to other parts of the country. A short while later, Domingo Cavallo offered his resignation as economy minister."[69]

THE DEFAULT

On Christmas Eve, Argentina defaulted, suspending payments on US$61.8 billion of public bonds and US$8 billion dollars of other debt instruments.[70] At that stage, however, the default excluded debt service repayments worth some US$32.4 billion, along with guaranteed loans of some US$42.3 billion to the likes of the IMF, the World Bank and the Inter-American Development Bank. Nevertheless, as Baer, Margot and Montes-Rojas observe, the default amounted to the largest ever default in Latin American economic history, affecting US$82 billion out of total debts outstanding of US$153 billion.

Freed from the straitjacket of the dollar peg, the Argentinean peso devalued sharply. While barred from access to trade credit, Argentina enjoyed a sharp increase in exports. Imports shrank, meanwhile, resulting in a near immediate balance-of-payments surplus. Agricultural commodities and industrial products became very attractively priced for overseas buyers. Thanks to the default, the government's deficit problems also eased, now that it no longer had to make such enormous interest payments.

At the same time, imports became hugely costly. This again had a tremendously positive impact on the country's trade balance. Moreover, by defaulting, one of the major causes of Argentina's massive public deficit – the country's huge interest payments on its debt – vanished instantly.[71] By 2002, Argentina had regained some price control over its exports and the margin earned by exporters started going up sharply. The economy improved by leaps and bounds, indeed perhaps too strongly. The overheating stoked rising inflation, which continues to be a major problem for Argentina today.

LESSONS FROM PAST CRISES

NOW THAT WE HAVE LOOKED at these earlier debt crises it is important to draw out the lessons we can learn from them.

The first is surely how rapidly a country's position can deteriorate towards default. Economic and financial difficulties can persist for years, without apparently creating serious problems in the eyes of the rest of the world, and then suddenly come to a head within days.

It is also clear that sovereign debt defaults and near-defaults are not an unusual phenomenon at all. As the extensive research of Carmen Reinhart and Kenneth Rogoff has ably demonstrated, these episodes have tended to occur very frequently over the last couple of centuries and longer. It is much easier for nations to amass debts than to find workable solutions to their underlying economic and financial shortcomings.

While we tend to talk of these crises as having come and gone, their consequences are often long-lasting. Disputes arising from a default can endure for years. There is a widespread belief that Argentina got away with the largest sovereign default in history in 2001. However, in April 2012, the Paris Club reiterated that if Argentina wanted access to credit again, it is still expected to repay Club members US$9bn within the next three years, being the $6.2bn upon which it defaulted as well as unpaid interest, beginning with a large initial payment in order to show willing.

In other words, unless there is a formal restructuring or debt forgiveness agreed by the defaulting country's creditors, the debts remain, accruing further interest. The price of rejoining the community of borrowers typically requires the defaulter to resume its responsibilities for its unpaid debts and related interest. So, while default might secure relief for a government for some time, it will ultimately have to restore its reputation the expensive way if it wants to regain its access to trade credit on reasonable terms.

The present situation

IN THE PRESENT CRISIS OF GOVERNMENT debt in the developed world, we should not focus exclusively on the risks of the sort of default we have examined here. Some defaults are more insidious than others, occurring by way of currency devaluation and inflation over time. While Britain is regarded as one of the safer bets in the world of sovereign debt, the UK authorities are already engaged in trying to shrink the value of its very substantial external debts by way of aggressive money printing. So far, international investors have not objected in any meaningful way, but there are growing concerns about where this may lead.

When a government finally repays a bond at maturity with a currency that it has caused to devalue for 20 years or more, the cost to that government is much lighter than it would otherwise have been. The bondholder, meanwhile, has suffered a substantial loss of purchasing power in their money. However, the effects have been spread out over a number of years, rather than imposed by way of a sudden and dramatic default.

Fear of the impact of the insidious effects of inflationary policies is a major reason for growing tensions between the Chinese authorities and its US counterpart. The Chinese have called for "responsible fiscal policies" and are vehemently opposed to further quantitative easing or money-printing by the US, as they fear that the result will be devaluation of their massive holdings of US Treasuries and other American assets.

With no government immune to the danger of default and leading Western economies such as the US and UK economy surreptitiously eroding their debt burden, investors need to recognise that even supposedly *risk-free* sovereign debt needs to be handled with care. While it may be held for short-term tactical reasons or as part of a balanced portfolio, the risks across the board are now greater than they have been for many decades.

ENDNOTES

[50] www.cato.org/pubs/journal/cj17n3-14.html

[51] José Julián Sidaoui's paper 'Policies for international reserve accumulation under a floating exchange rate regime: the experience of Mexico (1995-2003)' is available online (www.bis.org/publ/bppdf/bispap23r.pdf).

[52] Andrew Wheat, 'The fall of the Peso and the Mexican "Miracle" ', *Multinational Monitor*, (April 1995).

[53] Wheat, ibid.

[54] Jonathan Roeder and Nacha Cattan, 'Europe Should Learn From Mexican "Tequila Crisis," G-20 Host Tellez Says', Bloomberg (February 2012).

[55] Angeles Villareal, 'M. NAFTA and the Mexican Economy', Congressional Research Service (3 June 2010).

[56] Thomson Financial Datastream.

[57] Roeder and Cattan, 'Europe Should Learn From Mexican "Tequila Crisis," '.

[58] Mexico, Country Studies, Library of Congress, *countrystudies.us/mexico/66.htm*

[59] Gaidar, 'Lessons of the Russian Crisis for Transition Economies' (www.imf.org/external/pubs/ft/fandd/1999/06/pdf/gaidar.pdf).

[60] Gaidar, ibid.

[61] Gaidar, ibid.

[62] Abbigail Chiodo and Michael Owyan, 'A Case Study of a Currency Crisis: The Russian Default of 1998', The Federal Reserve Bank of St. Louis (2002), research.stlouisfed.org/publications/review/02/11/ChiodoOwyang.pdf

[63] Chiodo and Michael Owyan, 'A Case Study of a Currency Crisis', p. 6.

[64] Chiodo and Michael Owyan, ibid, p. 8.

[65] RIA Novosti, 'Russia's economy under Vladimir Putin: achievements and failures' (1 March 2008).

[66] Steve H. Hanke, 'Argentina's Boom and Bust', (**www.cato.org/publications/commentary/argentinas-boom-bust**).

[67] 'Argentina's central banker sacked', BBC (26 April 2001).

[68] David Litterick, The Telegraph (11 December 2001), **www.telegraph.co.uk/finance/economics/2745217/Argentina-bond-yields-hit-42pc.html**

[69] **news.bbc.co.uk/1/hi/world/americas/1720915.stm**

[70] Cited by Baer, Margot and Montes-Rojas, 'Argentina's Default and the Lack of Dire Consequences' p.11.

[71] Baer, Margot and Montes-Rojas, 'Argentina's Default'.

CHAPTER 6

THE FUTURE OF THE EURO

NO PAPER CURRENCY has ever stood the test of time. At least, that is the mantra of those who argue for a return to *sound* – or gold-backed – money. They have a point. Currencies backed by nothing but the word of the governments that issue them have repeatedly come and gone. At best, such a currency's value withers steadily over time and, at worst, collapses in spectacular fashion. Such a dramatic undoing potentially awaits the single European currency.

CONTEMPLATING A COLLAPSE OF THE EURO

THE COLLAPSE OF THE EURO would indeed be truly a spectacular occurrence. Never in the modern age has a currency of such standing gone out of existence, still less within a short few years of its creation. Typically, monetary failure has been confined to individual, economically undeveloped nations. Yet, there is a genuine risk that the currency presently used by several of the world's most important economies could soon join the Hungarian pengo and the Chilean escudo in the graveyard of failed currencies.

Just as the euro's demise would be unprecedented, so would the economic and financial consequences of such an event. It is, of course, hard to quantify exactly what these might be. What does seem likely, however, is that it would entail the destruction of wealth on a grand scale. The effects would surely be felt far beyond the eurozone's borders. For example, the single currency accounts for around a quarter of official global foreign exchange reserves.

Unprecedented crises can also spawn unique opportunities. One need only think back to the financial turmoil of 2008 for a good example of this. While the US housing crash and sub-prime mortgage fiasco directly and indirectly wiped out vast amounts of wealth, Paulson & Co. – the hedge fund run by John Paulson – reportedly reaped a $15 billion profit by correctly speculating on disaster. Notably, this fund correctly chose to ignore the authorities' repeated reassurances about the health of the market.

Naturally, a total collapse of the single European currency is only one possible outcome. It is conceivable that the euro will survive but undergo a significant change of membership, or a massive devaluation. The permutations are manifold and serve to deepen the uncertainty for investors. There are some excellent studies addressing the gamut of outcomes, including particularly worthy offerings from PricewaterhouseCoopers, the *Guardian* and FutureCompany.[72]

When exploring all the various outcomes, there is a danger of losing sight of the wood for the trees. It is worth taking a step back and examining a few fundamental issues, such as the forces that brought the euro into existence, the benefits it has delivered and whether these merit retaining it in its existing form. At the same time, we should also ponder whether it would be possible to wind back the clock to a Europe of sovereign currencies, and how European trade and competitiveness might look were this to happen.

TENSIONS WITHIN THE EUROZONE

POLITICAL WILL BEHIND THE EURO

THE POLITICAL WILL THAT CREATED the euro continues to shape the handling of the current crisis. None of the core eurozone countries – such as Germany, France or the Netherlands – has so far given any serious indication that they might give up on the currency. As such, the possibility of the euro disintegrating into 17 separate currencies still looks to be remote. It would probably only ever occur after a whole string of other solutions, such as the sort of *two-tier* currency union to which former President Sarkozy of France had alluded while still in office, had been tried and had failed.

HOW TO DEAL WITH THE EURO CRISIS

In the same way, the internal tensions that have long bedevilled European politics are also influencing the evolution of the euro crisis. Even before eurozone governments faced possible insolvency, there was fundamental disagreement over the policies that the European Central Bank (ECB) should pursue. The essence of this is whether the ECB should limit itself to keeping inflation under strict control or whether it should have a more expansive agenda of trying to promote growth and employment.

The main protagonists in this debate have always been Germany and France. The former has traditionally argued for prudent monetary policies, while the latter has long wanted the ECB to seek to stimulate job creation and be prepared to fund worthy social programmes, *worthy* equating to whatever the French government of the day deems to be so. These positions stem from Germany's deep-rooted fear of price instability following its hyperinflationary crisis during the interwar years, and France's record of tolerating inflation in return for other economic and social benefits.

EURO BONDS

This fundamental clash of philosophies has found its way into the current sovereign debt crisis in several ways. A classic example of this is the crucial debate surrounding the issuance of so-called euro bonds. France and others would like to see the creation of a single eurozone-wide bond that any member government could issue. A euro bond would potentially allow financially troubled nations such as Portugal and Ireland to borrow on much better terms than they can currently do on their own.

In recent times, the weakest members of the euro club have frequently found themselves forced to borrow at rates of interest far higher than Germany pays. This is in stark contrast to the experience of the first few years of the single currency's existence, where the interest rates paid by the various countries were generally very close to one another. It is argued that a euro bond would have a similar effect. Such a security would be jointly and severally guaranteed by all the member countries, irrespective of which country had issued it.

As Europe's largest and strongest economy, Germany fears that it would end up footing more than its fair share of the bill arising from the creation of euro bonds. Specifically, it sees itself being saddled with a disproportionate share of the large debts that the club's weaker members have run up and may continue to amass. As such, Germany is understandably reluctant to go down the road towards euro bonds, at least not until Portugal, Italy, Greece and Spain have shown the same sort of fiscal rectitude that Germany itself believes that it displays.

ECB BUYING GOVERNMENT BONDS

Failing the creation of a euro bond, France would like to see the ECB assuage the continent's debt crisis by directly investing in government debt. Printing money and using it to purchase government bonds has helped to lower state borrowing costs in the US, the UK, Japan and Switzerland. France argues that buying up, say, Portuguese or Greek debt would give those embattled countries precious time in which to put their finances in order and make much-needed improvements to productivity. This could also prevent the crisis spreading to other parts of the single-currency bloc in the meantime.

Once more, though, Germany has set its face against the ECB's purchasing government debt outright. Its concern is that such actions would serve to weaken the euro dramatically against other currencies, in turn stoking inflation. Rather than encouraging the eurozone's problem-children to mend their ways in a more comfortable timeframe, Germany fears that it could even instead promote further laxity. Nevertheless, quantitative easing may eventually prove inevitable if the single currency is to survive in its present form.

Admittedly, France's enthusiasm for resorting to quantitative easing was not shared by the Frenchman who formerly stood at the helm of the ECB. Jean-Claude Trichet was firmly wedded to the cause of price stability and stated repeatedly[73] in his final year in office that the ECB's greatest achievement over the past dozen years had been keeping inflation close to its target of two per cent. His successor seems less zealous to date, however. The Italian Mario Draghi has adopted a rather more nuanced approach, steering a middle way between German doctrinal rigidity and French urges to crank up the printing presses.

LENDING TO EUROPEAN BANKS

Mr Draghi's solution has been to lend huge amounts to Europe's banks for three-year periods at extremely low or zero rates of interest. In the first months of 2012, this programme has seen more than €2 trillion pumped into the continent's troubled banking system. Mr Draghi appears to have an unofficial understanding with the banks: the ECB will provide them with much needed funds in return for which the banks will invest a large portion of the proceeds in eurozone government bonds. The banks then offer these bonds back to the ECB as collateral for further loans. The ECB accepts them as collateral at such a price as to help keep their issuers' borrowing costs low.

This arrangement appears to achieve the kind the results that France wants but without arousing Germany's antipathy to money printing. After all, the ECB is not technically engaging in the most direct approach of buying sovereign debt itself. It has, however, vastly swollen the ECB's balance sheet, in the form of all the collateral it has accepted from Europe's banks. However, since that collateral is accepted and then held at current market prices, the ECB is able to go back to the banks and ask for more – and different – collateral as and when the need arises.

The project has been a resounding success, as of late March 2012. Financial markets have responded very positively to what Mr Draghi's ECB has done. Borrowing costs for several European countries have come down substantially, while equities have rallied impressively during the first quarter of 2012, both in Europe and elsewhere, particularly in the US. It is still early days, however, and there are obvious risks involved. Not least of these is that Europe's banks could run out of acceptable collateral very quickly if the sovereign debt they have provided to the ECB were to decline rapidly in value.

Although rising equity markets create an obvious feel-good factor, they are no panacea for the underlying – and still ongoing – crisis of government debt. To resolve this crisis definitively, Europe needs to achieve sustained economic growth and improve the state of its various governments' finances. But there is an obvious conflict between the two goals. It is hard for Europe to achieve economic growth while governments simultaneously lay off large numbers of employees in order to save money. Rising unemployment saps consumer spending and in turn stymies economic growth.

DIVERGENT COMPETITIVENESS WITHIN THE EUROZONE

Sharply contrasting competitiveness is another of the deeply rooted tensions within the eurozone. There is a huge gulf in this respect between some of the core eurozone members, such as Germany and Holland, and some of those on its periphery, including Portugal, Greece and Spain. PricewaterhouseCoopers – the global accountancy giant – sums up the problem thus:

> *"Over the last decade, there has also been a divergence of competitiveness between countries running a current account surplus and countries running a deficit .... The sizable and persistent imbalance has been supported by a complementary flow of credit from the surplus countries to the deficit countries. This has enabled a build up in public and private debt, delayed a correction in competitiveness and allowed the structural problems of the eurozone to be hidden."*

To see what this means in practice, consider labour costs across the eurozone. The real cost of labour in Italy, Greece and Spain has risen substantially since the year 2000, whereas that in Germany has come down. This gives Germany and other core euro nations a key advantage in terms of production costs. The only cure for this structural flaw is for the peripheral nations to endure the painful process of forcing down real wages in their countries.

While extremely painful, reducing real wages is possible. Greece – the most uncompetitive of the lot – has already made significant strides in this regard. As of early 2012, it has driven down wages by some 11 per cent over the last year or so. In its March 2012 report on Greece, the International Monetary Fund (IMF) highlighted the progress made – but also the exact process by which the country had got itself into such difficulties to begin with.

After joining the euro in 2001, Greece's private sector almost doubled its debt-load relative to the size of the country's economy. The government also increased its indebtedness substantially, from around 100 per cent of the size of the economy to around 130 per cent. The extra spending was not put to good use. Instead, it went to bolstering the country's famously generous social benefits, including pensions for early retirees. Wages rose much faster than the rate of productivity growth, while Greek inflation ran beyond the level of most of its trading partners. Locked into the single European currency, Greece's competitiveness deteriorated by around 20 to 30 per cent.

Although the situation persisted for some years, it was never ultimately going to be sustainable. Bond investors had been willing to take a relaxed view of Greece's deliberate understatement of its indebtedness and its other rule-bending that had enabled it to enter the single currency in the first place. The credit crunch that first bit in 2007 has laid these problems bare, however. In subsequent years, it became painfully obvious that Greece could not afford to refinance its massive debts at the rates that the market was now demanding.

To avoid defaulting on its debts, Greece has had to rely on bailouts from its European Union peers. This vital support has come at a high price, however. Both the EU and the IMF have insisted that Greece make deep and extremely painful cuts to its bloated public spending. They have also registered their displeasure at the country's lack of progress in raising money from selling off state-owned assets. The Greek government has struggled to obtain approval for these measures in parliament. For a week or so in 2011, it was literally touch-and-go as to whether they would be passed.

The lesson of this episode is that financial markets can lose patience very rapidly indeed; a change of attitude can occur quite literally overnight. Naturally, this serves to focus the minds of politicians rather nicely. After many months of wrangling and hesitation, Greece's lawmakers have so far managed to do what the markets required of them, albeit only in the nick of time. However, there is a very real danger that at some point, they will fail to do so, with potentially cataclysmic consequences for markets everywhere.

SPREAD OF CONTAGION THROUGHOUT THE EU

NOTHING DEMONSTRATES THIS point more starkly than the history of the spread of contagion in the wider European Union. Having taken fright at Greece, the markets looked anew at the position of other EU states. They quickly noticed that Portugal and Ireland were in almost as poor financial shape as Greece. Both these countries' borrowing costs soared rapidly to the point where they too needed to be bailed out. The effects spread to Italy and Spain, with the latter the main cause for concern as of late March 2012. Even France has now been mentioned as a possible victim of contagion.[74]

A full-blown panic involving either Italy or Spain would stretch the eurozone's resources to their limits. Italy is the world's eighth largest economy and Spain the twelfth largest. Bailing out just one of these countries would be cripplingly expensive for the rest of the EU. Merely to buy time in order for the eurozone to put its house in order could cost up €1.5 trillion ($2 trillion), according to some estimates. Thus far, the EU has only managed to come up with a fund that totals around half that amount.

THE EFSF AND THE ESM

The fund as it is mooted at present consists of two elements. The European Financial Stability Facility (EFSF) was set up in May 2010 with a mandate to safeguard financial stability in Europe by providing financial assistance to troubled peripheral countries. It has the ability to issue bonds and other debt instruments in the capital markets, which are guaranteed by eurozone member states. The EFSF has so far provided some €200 billion in aid and has a top-notch credit rating from two of the three main credit rating agencies.

However, the EFSF was always seen as a temporary vehicle, to be replaced in due course by a permanent fund called the European

Stability Mechanism (ESM). The ESM was to be funded by all 17 member states in the euro, in proportion to their funding ratios to the European Central Bank. There was a great deal of wrangling over both the ideal size of the ESM and whether or not it should run alongside the EFSF for a while or simply take over its obligations.

Germany in particular wanted the ESM to be as small as possible and for its overall funding to include the EFSF. The markets, and to some degree France, wanted the fund to be as large as possible and for the total sum to be boosted by the EU agreeing to allow the EFSF to continue alongside the ESM. Thanks to relentless pressure from financial markets, it is the latter option that has been selected. On Friday 30 March 2012, the Austrian Finance Minister Maria Fekter announced that the ESM, which is due to come into operation in mid-2012, will have €500 billion at its disposal and that this figure will be in addition to the €200 billion in aid issued by the EFSF.

Prior to this announcement, Germany's Chancellor Angela Merkel and her finance minister Wolfgang Schäuble had vigorously argued that the permanent rescue fund's €500 billion should incorporate the €200 billion of loans that the EFSF had already made. However, the ESM will also now include some €100 billion in aid given to Greece in 2010, bringing the total figure up to €800 billion. France's then finance minister François Baroin had wanted the fund to be €1 trillion, arguing that it was "a little like the nuclear option in military planning, there for dissuasion, not to be used." The Organisation for Economic Cooperation and Development (OECD) had earlier made much the same point, advising the EU to opt for a "firewall" of €1 trillion.

Of course, if the fund were to be called on to provide anything more than a modest bailout to Italy or Spain, financial markets would hardly be soothed. A massive obligation would then fall upon France and Germany, which would sorely affect their credit ratings and drive up their borrowing costs, thereby spreading, rather than preventing, contagion. The ideal solution, from the EU's perspective, would be for the ESM to receive very substantial pledges from non-EU sources.

SUPPORT FROM OUTSIDE THE EU

Both China and Japan in particular have a major interest in the euro not collapsing into chaos. The EU is one of their major trading partners and the impact on world trade of an EU collapse would be profound. To date, both countries have indicated some willingness to support the EU, but only once the most badly affected EU states have made further progress in addressing their structural flaws.

As to the form that such support might take, one possibility is that China and Japan buy the bonds of eurozone nations, helping to lower their borrowing costs. There is some evidence of the involvement in certain eurozone bond markets of significant mystery buyers, which may mean that this process is already underway by stealth. Alternatively, China and Japan could make a direct pledge of funds to the ESM or, alternatively, substantially increase their contributions to the IMF.

In any event, there are growing signs that both China and Japan may be willing to back the eurozone with hard cash at some point in the not too distant future. During high-level talks between the two East Asian giants early in 2012, the pair agreed to co-operate closely over the issue of providing additional funding to the IMF. As the world's second and third largest economies respectively, China and Japan may have found themselves competing for the prestige of pledging the most to the IMF. The agreement to co-operate on the scale of their contributions gets around this, but it also signals a warming of relations between two of the EU's three biggest trading partners (the US being the third).

According to Reuters, the IMF is seeking some €600 billion in additional funding from member countries in order to boost its capacity for providing emergency assistance. The EU has not been slow to inform the IMF that, having managed to establish an €800 billion fund itself, it now also wants the IMF to provide a substantial package of support to complement the EU's new and enhanced firewall.

In November 2011, the IMF announced that it was expanding its global credit facility, namely its precautionary credit line (PCL), which aims to provide support to member countries over periods of one to two years. This expansion now makes it possible for member countries facing very short-term liquidity difficulties to borrow for just six months at a time. The PCL is not eurozone specific, but it can be applied to the eurozone.

The IMF's new credit line, called the *precautionary and liquidity line*, allows governments to apply for a loan of up to a maximum of five times the relevant country's financial contribution to the IMF. Assuming that Italy qualified for the PCL, it would have access to some $60 billion of IMF funding on top of any bailout funding it gets from the EU, should it require it. The idea of calming markets by amassing a huge reserve fund does nothing, however, to address the deep-seated structural flaws of the eurozone's most troubled members.

EUROZONE MEMBERS ADDRESSING INTERNAL PROBLEMS

THERE IS TANGIBLE EVIDENCE that some of the worst hit peripheral states are making headway in reducing their budget deficits. For example, Ireland has already achieved a fiscal adjustment equivalent to 13 per cent of the total size of its economy.[75] The nation has also managed to cut wages in its public sector by 15 per cent over the last three years, according to Alan

Ahearne from the National University of Ireland, Galway. As well as enjoying an improvement in exports, Portugal is targeting structural fiscal adjustments amounting to nine per cent of GDP by 2013.

Spain – one of the larger problem cases – is still suffering from the implosion of its real-estate bubble, which has left its banking sector in a damaged state. Spain ran a budget deficit equivalent to eight per cent of GDP in 2011, compared to a targeted deficit of six per cent. However, the country has established a new constitutional rule that prevents the growth of government spending exceeding growth in the economy as a whole. The authorities now believe that Spain is on course to achieve the EU target of a fiscal budget of less than three per cent of GDP by 2013.

Italy, meanwhile, is in even better shape. Guntram Wolff, the deputy director of the think tank Bruegel, says that whereas net external liabilities for Greece and Portugal are currently in excess of 100 per cent of GDP, with Ireland not far below that level, Italy's net external liabilities are currently within 20 per cent of GDP. While the Italian state has amassed hulking debts, this is substantially offset by the large asset holdings of the country's households. What is more, the country's banking system has not lent heavily to any of the other four troubled peripheral nations.

In fact, Italy's main problem is probably one of guilt by association. Due to its weakening – albeit not disastrous – exports and competitiveness, Italy tends to be lumped together with the likes of Spain. "For Italy, most economists would probably agree, there is no solvency issue unless the market is driving up the interest rate, thereby triggering a self-fulfilling liquidity-solvency crisis," says Wolff.[76]

It is not really possible to identify what would set this process in motion, however. Financial markets can tolerate problems such as those of Italy for long periods and then take fright just like that. Having explored the history of state indebtedness over a 200-year period, Carmen Reinhart and Kenneth Rogoff concluded that there is no signal that consistently occurs in advance of a sudden and catastrophic loss of market confidence.[77] An out-of-the-blue spike in borrowing costs can therefore force a highly indebted government into default overnight.

It is surely with this in mind that the European Union's ESM bailout fund was created; its presence is meant to reassure financial markets and thereby prevent a sudden and ruinous bout of nerves. In a case where the markets were to really lose faith though, the ESM is likely to get washed away in its entirety like a sandcastle in the face of spring tides. This was the point made by Germany's Finance Minister, Wolfgang Schäuble, when he said: "There is no [bailout] sum with which you can convince markets. You can only be convincing with structural measures."

The formidable Schäuble has been sorely tested by the EU crisis. Both he and Chancellor Angela Merkel have consistently promised that Germany's obligations in supporting the currency union would be strictly limited, but without spooking financial markets. However, members of the German Parliament have frequently accused this duo of crossing the very *red lines* that they promised they would not.

ASSESSING A RETURN TO SOVEREIGN CURRENCIES

Nobody can pretend that there is not a continuing risk to the single European currency, either from further sudden losses of market confidence, or from the possible election of new governments on a platform of leaving the euro. While this could conceivably occur in one of the eurozone's stronger member countries, it is surely most likely in the weaker states. For the likes of Greece and Portugal in particular, the idea of returning to a sovereign currency and improving their competitiveness via devaluation rather than wage cuts has obvious appeal.

At the same time, however, there is also an understanding in the most troubled nations that abandoning the euro could create problems at least as serious as those from which they are already suffering. Newly restored sovereign currencies would almost inevitably plunge immediately against the euro. This would leave those countries unable to service their debts, which would continue to be denominated in their former currency. Defaulting on those debts would make it extremely difficult for them to borrow from outsiders for many years to come. This could force even more painful cuts in public spending than are currently occurring.

In this situation, the troubled ex-euro members would probably have to turn to the IMF for assistance. The IMF has a long record of providing aid to financially distressed nations and prescribing and overseeing the necessary economic reforms. Admittedly, this process is seldom painless for the average citizen of the countries in question, as the current experience of Greece shows so vividly.

To most Greeks, the austerity measures that the outside world has forced upon them have caused enormous pain, but with little obvious gain, at least so far. It is essential that both the eurozone as a whole and the governments of the weakest members like Greece demonstrate that they can improve competitiveness, enact structural reforms and restore fiscal health. Whether this is achievable before either the markets or a majority of the voting public lose patience remains to be seen.

In the event that one or more of the peripheral member-countries is either forced out of the eurozone or chooses to leave, financial markets in the eurozone and beyond will surely experience havoc for some time. The economic uncertainty and dislocation would be immense. Years of legal wrangling could ensue, as those who struck contracts in euro found themselves faced with payment in a vastly devalued, lesser currency. The value of equities, bonds and real estate in any exiting nation would also be likely to tumble dramatically, both in the build-up to the event and thereafter. The fallout would be felt across the rest of the eurozone and beyond.

How investors can play the eurozone situation

In an environment of chaos, the main priority of most investors would be to protect their existing wealth, rather than to grow it. However, as John Paulson's experience during the financial meltdown of 2008 demonstrated, there will be big opportunities for those able and brave enough to exploit them. This would involve both minimising one's exposure to certain areas, while simultaneously taking more adventurous positions in others.

High-yield corporate bonds

European high-yield corporate bonds would doubtless prove especially vulnerable to the sort of market turbulence that would follow a partial disintegration of the eurozone. High-yield bonds have done exceedingly well over the last two years and have attracted a very substantial inflow of capital, with many institutions and high-net-worth individuals allocating greater proportions of their portfolios to this area. But holders of such bonds issued by companies in a country departing the single currency would almost certainly suffer a lethal combination of plunging capital values and massive exchange-rate losses. This segment of the bond market would therefore be an obvious one to avoid.

Position oneself early

Positioning oneself as early as possible would surely be essential. Although the potential disaster has been many years in the making, an implosion of the eurozone would occur with alarming speed. Any nation planning to abandon the single currency would inevitably have to take steps to prevent capital from fleeing its banks and financial markets. One of its first measures, therefore, would be the imposition of restrictions on capital exports, such as those imposed by Argentina during its crisis that we discussed in Chapter 5. Citizens of the most vulnerable nations as well as foreigners owning bank accounts in those nations should consider switching their savings to another jurisdiction.

Citizens and authorities of certain troubled nations may already be preparing discreetly for this. In April 2012, Spain's recently-elected government announced a new measure obliging Spaniards to disclose to the authorities any foreign bank accounts and any other overseas asset holdings that they might have.[78] The stated purpose of this measure was to minimise tax evasion, but it could clearly also double as a future means of impeding funds from the leaving the country and also perhaps even of forcing citizens to repatriate savings and other wealth.

SHORT-SELLING

Short-selling shares and other publicly-traded instruments in the eurozone's most vulnerable countries offers one way to try and profit from a future euro exit. Shorting continental banks could be particularly worthwhile. The European Central Bank's LTRO programme has encouraged banks in the peripheral states to add to the holdings of their own governments' debt, which thereby increases those banks' exposure to a sovereign default. And the shockwaves would likely extend to the stocks of financial institutions in surviving eurozone countries too.

LOOK TO THE STRONGER ECONOMIES

In an even more extreme scenario of total eurozone disintegration, where even the likes of Germany reverted to a national currency, assets in those stronger countries would surely significantly outperform those in the weaker ones. Put simply, investors would flee stocks in the peripheral nations and embrace those in the core. A restored Deutsche Mark would have much of the safe-haven appeal of the Swiss franc, while German equities could do especially well in relative terms, although not necessarily in absolute ones.

Of course, were the Deutsche Mark restored, its likely appreciation against many other currencies would surely hurt the competitiveness of German exporters. These firms have enjoyed a bonanza in recent years, thanks to the euro being rather cheaper than German economic fundamentals really justified. Saddled with a strong currency once more, their businesses could suffer for a time, which could in turn hinder their share price performance. However, with so much capital from elsewhere seeking a stable home, shares in blue-chip giants like SAP and Siemens could still prosper, despite the currency headwinds.

THE MOST LIKELY OUTCOME

As responsible investors, it is only right that we should have a clear idea of what strategies we might follow were the eurozone to break-up either fully or partly. However, it is also worth bearing in mind that a break-up is not the most likely outcome. The political will that helped bring about the euro in the first place remains incredibly strong. The desire of today's political leaders to see the single-currency project succeed should eventually override other national sensibilities, even Germany's antipathy to inflationary policies. Sooner or later, the ECB will probably pursue the money-printing and bond-buying policies that its counterparts elsewhere have already successfully deployed. A weaker euro will be more palatable for Europe and for the world than no euro at all.

ENDNOTES

[72] 'What next for Eurozone?', PwC, **www.pwc.co.uk/economic-services/publicatio ns/what-next-for-eurozone-potential-outcomes-2012.jhtml**

[73] In an interview with the BIS on 20 April 2011, Trichet said: "We are proud of the fact that during the first 12 years of the euro we have delivered price stability, in line with our definition, namely 'below 2%, but close to, 2%'. To be precise, we have delivered an average yearly price increase to our 331 million fellow citizens of 1.97%. And it is extremely important to continue solidly anchoring inflation expectations in a period which is marked by uncertainties and turbulences." **www.bis.org/review/r110426a.pdf**

[74] The decision by the ratings agency Standard & Poor's to strip France of its triple-A rating on Friday 13 January 2012 can itself be viewed as symptomatic of the "contagion", with the ratings agencies themselves being caught up in, and frequently exacerbating the ebbing of market confidence.

[75] Peterson Institute and Bruegel, 'Resolving the European Debt Crisis'.

[76] The full report, 'Resolving the European Debt Crisis' is available from the Peterson Institute (**bookstore.piie.com/book-store/6420.html**). The chapter by Wolff, 'The Euro Area Crisis: Policy Options Ahead', is available as a free PDF download from that page.

[77] 'This Time is Different: A Panoramic View of Eight Centuries of Financial Crises'.

[78] 'El Gobierno español controlará las cuentas bancarias en el extranjero', **Deia.com** (13 April 2012).

CHAPTER 7

FEAR AND LOATHING ON WALL STREET

IF YOU ARE READING THIS BOOK in 2012, I hope that you are particularly enjoying the experience. After all, it could very easily be the last volume that you ever peruse. At some point this year, perhaps in late December, the world is due to come to an end. That, at least, is the quirky prediction that some modern-day folk have managed to tease out of their selective reading of an ancient Mesoamerican calendar. (If you are reading this after 2012, either you are to be congratulated for surviving the Apocalypse or the prediction was flawed.)

This latest forecast of the earth's imminent expiry is one of the more light-hearted examples of a popular neurosis that has become ever more prevalent in the early 21st century. Every few weeks or months, a new public fear erupts, typically concerning some cataclysmic event or process. Terrorism, unconventional warfare, natural disaster and pandemic disease have all enjoyed stints as the dark obsession of the day. This tendency seems to carry through to the financial markets and have an acute effect there too.

Theory has it that financial markets are made up of cool, calculating investors who make decisions based on cold, hard facts alone. The reality, of course, is often very different. Markets are inherently prone to fads. Every era in financial history has played host to at least one short-lived craze, usually more, be it for technology companies, some hot new derivative instrument, or a new valuation method. Each enjoys 15 minutes of fame before being consigned to obscurity or notorious shame. This faddishness extends also to fear.

THE FAD FOR FEAR

OF COURSE, FEAR IS HARDLY a new phenomenon in financial markets. Along with its partner-in-crime – greed – fear has long been anecdotally acknowledged as a major force in moving the prices of traded assets. In recent decades, the school of behavioural finance has made significant progress in explaining how emotions cause markets to behave as they do, but fairly little has been said about the specific fearfulness that has characterised the last few years.

It is worth our while to try and understand the fad for fear. If it is irrational, it may offer us investment opportunities. If it is mere noise that has no real bearing on markets, we may be able to train ourselves to block it out and focus instead on what really matters. In order to get to grips with this phenomenon, we need therefore to explore the nature of the fearfulness.

THE TERRORIST ATTACKS OF 11 SEPTEMBER 2001

The fad for fear has become most noticeable since 11 September 2001. The terrorist attacks on the United States on that day were clearly one of the defining events of our generation. Everyone remembers where they were at the moment they heard the news that two airliners had crashed into the twin towers of the World Trade Centre. The explosions and the towers' subsequent collapse was more than just the most dramatic newsreel footage of the 21st century. The attacks had a psychological effect on people who were continents away from New York that day.

In the immediate aftermath of the atrocity, two in every five Americans are estimated to have suffered significant symptoms of stress. Ivy Tso and other researchers at the University of Michigan conducted a study assessing the brain activity of members of the general public in response to images of the 9/11 attacks. The stress and anxiety that their brain activity exhibited was far above normal and similar in nature – although not in severity – to those suffering from post-traumatic stress disorder.[79]

Post-traumatic stress disorder (PTSD) is a common condition that is brought on by a terrifying experience. Soldiers involved in front-line combat frequently suffer from PTSD, but it also affects those who are witnesses to distressing scenes, such as domestic violence, accidents and disasters. The symptoms of PTSD include anger, sleeping problems, flashbacks to the event and hyper-vigilance. Sufferers often also believe their futures will be constrained in ways not normal to other people.[80] In up to one-third of cases, the affliction can be life-long, especially where reminders of the trauma are recurring.

THE LEGACY OF THE ATTACKS

Although the attacks are more than a decade behind us today, their legacy is still very much with us. The War on Terror that the US launched in response to the atrocity is ongoing as of early 2012. Operations in Afghanistan, Pakistan and Iraq are estimated to have cost more than 236,000 lives, mainly civilians in those countries, but also those of more than 8,000 US servicemen and contractors. The financial cost to the United States – including additional future healthcare – is thought to be in the region of $3 to $4 trillion.[81] This is to say nothing of the human and financial costs incurred by allies of the US, such as the UK and Australia.

Even for those who choose to ignore the constant media coverage of the post-9/11 conflicts, there are other more practical reminders of that day. This doesn't just go for Americans, either. Travelling almost anywhere in the world by air is the most obvious example. Every time we have to queue for half an hour at airport security and then remove our shoes to be x-rayed, we become participants in this climate of heightened suspicion and fear, whether we wish to or not.

Politicians and the media have played critical roles in promoting the post-9/11 culture of fear, albeit not necessarily for the same reasons. For politicians, the aftermath of the attacks presented an opportunity to consolidate and extend the power of the state. Well over a hundred nations around the world enacted laws and other measures – including unprecedented levels of cross-border co-operation – with the stated aim of fighting terrorist financing.[82] The new rules, coincidentally, have made it much easier for governments to monitor and control the financial activities of every last citizen, rather than simply those of would-be jihadis.

Aside from those in the media who support the War on Terror for ideological reasons, newspapers and broadcasters have been eager peddlers of terrorism scares since 9/11. It is a truism that bad news sells better than good news and dramatic bad news – of which the attacks on New York and Washington were the most gruesomely vivid instance – can be the best sellers of all. As we will see shortly, the media has contributed enormously to the string of scares that have occurred over the past decade or so.

The 9/11 atrocity was undeniably a very real event indeed. Many of its subsequent effects – such as the War on Terror – have been equally real. But these events have clearly affected people's state of mind too. We have already discussed how among the symptoms of Post-Traumatic Stress Disorder are hyper-vigilance and a belief that one's future will be constrained in unusual ways. This describes many people's outlook in the post-9/11 Western world very well and it may apply especially well to the financial community.

THE IMPACT ON THE FINANCE INDUSTRY

The finance industry was on the front line of the 9/11 attacks. The World Trade Center stood just a couple of blocks from the heart of Wall Street. Investment workers were killed in large numbers. Among the towers' occupants who lost employees that day were household-name financial firms including the American Stock Exchange, Cantor Fitzgerald, Citigroup, Credit Suisse, Deutsche Bank, Merrill Lynch, Morgan Stanley, TD Waterhouse and UBS. To many employees of these firms – both in the US and in their many offices worldwide – it felt like they personally had come under attack.

The immediate financial fallout from the atrocity was dramatic, both in the US and internationally. Following the early-morning strike on the twin towers, the New York Stock Exchange did not open for business and remained closed for the next three days, its longest shutdown since the banking crisis of 1933. In London, the FTSE 100 index dropped 7.6 per cent on 11 September alone. The MSCI World Index – which covers developed markets around the globe – shed 14 per cent between 11 and 21 September.

While spectacular, the selling was also short-lived. After collapsing into 21 September, equities rallied strongly thereafter. America's S&P 500 index had recovered to where it had closed on 10 September within 13 trading sessions of the attacks and the trend remained broadly upwards for stocks until December. Despite this sharp but temporary bounce, the initial signs of the psychological damage to society also became apparent at exactly this time. The fad for fear was beginning in earnest.

THE ANATOMY OF A SCARE

It is worth pausing for a moment to explore briefly the nature of a scare. In 2007, Christopher Booker and Dr Richard North, two British writers, co-authored a study of the true cost of the efforts to deal with what they saw as some of the major public health scares of the day, including passive smoking, salmonella and climate change. In their book, they propose that a scare consists of seven basic attributes.[83]

According to Booker and North, a scare occurs when a genuine problem becomes blown up out of proportion, typically when it gets incorrectly lumped together with an unrelated issue. The scare must receive some endorsement from scientists or other perceived experts. It needs to be universal, such that almost anyone could be affected by the purported problem. It also has to be in some way new and mysterious, allowing for speculation to run wild. The media must then promote the scare, and the crisis arrives when the government acknowledges it. Finally, the truth begins to emerge.

The scares addressed by Booker and North were slightly different from the ones that have spooked financial markets since 9/11. The latter have tended to focus specifically on what might be described as apocalyptic outcomes, particularly involving warfare and pestilence. Further, whereas many of the scares that Booker and North chronicled have lasted many months or even years, the markets' bouts of apocalyptic dread have come and gone within a few weeks or days.

ANTHRAX AND BIOLOGICAL WARFARE SCARE

THE FIRST SHORT-LIVED SCARE of this variety following 9/11 occurred within a week or so. With America still in an entirely understandable state of shock from the unprecedented – and still only partly explained – attacks, a series of media organisations and two leading politicians received letters containing spores of anthrax. Around 20 or so people developed infections related to anthrax, five of whom died. Some of the letters contained what were supposed to be anti-US, anti-Israel and pro-Islamic slogans.

The anthrax campaign certainly succeeded in striking terror into the hearts of many ordinary Americans. Panic buying of survival equipment was reported in the US, including floods of requests for so-called 'NBC' or nuclear-biological-chemical suits. This fear spread far beyond America's borders; on the other side of the Atlantic, army surplus stores in Britain were reported as having sold out of gas masks.[84]

The media and assorted experts were quick to give credence to the anthrax scare even before the deadly mail campaign began. The first anthrax letters were postmarked Trenton, New Jersey, on 18 September. Between 11 and 18 September, there were 40 references to *bioterrorism* in United States news sources, up from five the week before the attacks, some of them shrilly sensational in their tone.

In a particularly prominent example, the *Washington Post* ran a feature-length piece on 17 September entitled 'Bioterrorism: an even more devastating threat'. The long word article opened with a description of how a small private plane could be used to infect tens of thousands of people with deadly viruses. It quoted an academic researcher of infectious diseases who warned that the threat from bioterrorism was many times greater than that of conventional attacks. It concluded by noting the nation's complete lack of preparedness for this new age of man-made plague and offered no balance whatsoever.[85]

The authorities were quick to add their warnings of the new risk of chemical and biological warfare. On 23 September, the Federal Bureau of Investigation (FBI) ordered that all crop-spraying light aircraft be grounded for 24 hours after a story broke alleging that Al-Qaeda operatives had shown interest in acquiring such planes, supposedly intending to distribute deadly viruses over US cities.[86]

THE REACTION OF THE FINANCIAL MEDIA AND THE MARKETS

The financial media took up the unconventional warfare theme just as enthusiastically as their mainstream counterparts. A headline in the *Wall Street Journal Europe* on 19 September claimed "Chemical, biological threat looms larger for US."[87] It also identified a sudden enthusiasm for buying into companies and industries that stood to benefit from the threat of society's latest and darkest fear.

Aside from the makers of military hardware and the providers of security services, investors piled heavily into companies in the pharmaceutical and biotechnology industry around this time. Stocks from this sector fell by less than the rest of the market in the wake of the attacks and then outperformed as the markets rallied. In the UK, for example, the FTSE 350 Pharmaceutical and Biotechnology sector fell 5.8 per cent from 10 to 21 September, compared to a 12.5 per cent fall for the UK market as a whole. As equities then recovered, pharmaceuticals continued to outpace the broader index.

The logic for buying into pharmaceuticals was fuzzy at best, however. Only a few companies stood to gain any direct benefit from a full-blown episode of bioterrorism and even then probably only to a modest extent. Germany's Bayer, for example, saw a massive increase in sales of Cipro, its treatment for anthrax. Its share price briefly outperformed its local stock market index from around the time of the outbreak of the scare into mid-October.

On the other hand, Acambis – a small British biotechnology firm – did receive a $428m order from the US government to produce a smallpox vaccine for every American citizen. Its share price more than doubled from £1.21p on the eve of 9/11 to £2.89 by 26 October. This case was definitely the exception rather than the rule however.

Besides the short-lived spurt in pharmaceutical and biotechnology shares, the transience of the anthrax scare in the markets is evident in how much attention the financial media gave to the subject. In the weeks immediately after the virus-laced letters were sent out, there was a huge spike in references to anthrax in financial publications around the world. As Chart 7.1 shows, this surge of interest drained away rapidly after October, although it did remain somewhat above the typical levels seen before the anthrax attacks.

CHART 7.1 – ANTHRAX IN THE FINANCIAL MEDIA, 2001 TO 2002

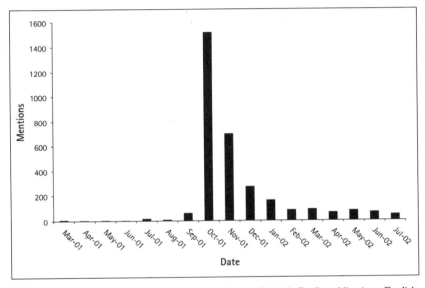

Source: Factiva: Bank & Credit publications, English,
all regions Search: Bank & Credit publications, English, all companies

As the bioterrorism scare faded into the background, investors refocused their anxieties on more traditional sources of risk. The massive bankruptcies of two corporate titans – Enron and Global Crossing – as well as the weakness of the US economy preoccupied the markets for much of 2002. However, the next apocalyptic scare for the world's financial markets was already incubating, this time many miles from Wall Street.

SARS

IN NOVEMBER 2002, a merchant was taken ill with a mystery virus in Foshun, in China's Guangdong province. Soon after his admission to hospital, several health workers contracted the illness too. It then spread to hundreds of other people living in the surrounding areas. Aside from flu-like symptoms, those infected also displayed difficulties in breathing. The Chinese authorities said nothing about the epidemic during its earliest stages, while Guangdong residents tried desperately to buy vinegar, which was rumoured to offer a cure for this new plague.

What came to be called Severe Acute Respiratory Syndrome (SARS) soon spread beyond the Guangdong province. Cases were reported in Hong Kong, Singapore, Vietnam, Thailand and also in Canada. It passed from person to person via coughs and sneezes, as well as other physical contact. Around a fifth of those infected were healthcare staff whose work had brought them close to sufferers. Worldwide, some 8,096 people were infected in total between November 2002 and July 2003, just under ten per cent of whom died.

SARS met all the criteria for a scare according to the model proposed by Booker and North. It was certainly novel and mysterious in terms of disease, and the Chinese authorities' initial attempts to suppress the facts of the outbreak only made it more so. It also spread rapidly to many countries, thereby highlighting that almost everyone was a potential victim. Governments apart from China's quickly acknowledged the problem and the media gave the story ample – and occasionally somewhat alarmist – airing.

The early publicity over SARS coincided with the build-up to the US and allied invasion of Iraq. On 14 March, while the story was still in its infancy, the BBC ran a piece written by a leading surgeon working at a hospital in Hong Kong. Professor Andrew Burd ended his op-ed contribution by saying: "We are at war but our enemy has no name, no identity. This reality easily eclipses the nightmare fantasies of Bush and Saddam. For the moment, Iraq is no longer an issue in Hong Kong."[88]

An even more chilling expert warning came from Dr Patrick Dixon of the Development Management School in London. He warned that there was a 25 per cent chance of SARS becoming a global pandemic, estimating that it could infect more than one billion people in a year. An Australian newspaper picked up this doom-laden prediction under the headline "Worse than Aids".[89]

Whilst SARS was indeed a real illness, the truth of the matter was more prosaic than that which the media had bandied about. The main problem was the lack of context offered. When viewed in isolation, the global death toll of 774 people does sound dramatic. However, this total covered numerous countries over many months. In the US, deaths related to ordinary, seasonal flu have averaged some 29,916 annually between 1976 and 2007.[90] On that basis, the number of victims claimed by SARS in 2002 to 2003 around the world is rather less alarming.

HOW THE FINANCIAL MARKETS WERE AFFECTED

Still, SARS undoubtedly had an impact on financial markets at the time. This was largely concentrated in Southeast Asia, the region most affected by the virus. The Hong Kong stock market underperformed America's S&P 500 by 15.8 per cent between early March and late April 2003, with Singaporean equities underperforming by 9.9 per cent, and Chinese stocks lagging by 9.3 per cent. Travel and tourism-related stocks were especially hard hit, with Asian hotels underperforming world equities by 20.3 per cent, and Asian airlines underperforming by 23.5 per cent.[91]

While stock markets rallied convincingly in the US and Europe around this time, many investors – particularly private ones – missed out. The mood affecting many of them was summed up by the widely respected commentator Stephen Roach of Morgan Stanley, who predicted a worldwide recession in 2003, describing SARS as the "final nail in the coffin."[92]

The spread of SARS had fizzled out by the early summer of 2003. The "worse than AIDS" pandemic was clearly not to be and press references shrivelled away accordingly. As can be seen in Chart 7.2, the presence of SARS in the media rose sharply in early 2003 but had fallen away again – albeit not entirely – halfway through the year.

CHART 7.2 – RISE AND FALL OF SARS IN THE NEWS

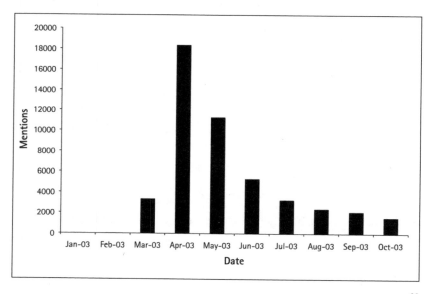

Source: Factiva[93]

Despite the failure of SARS to become the 21st century's first global plague, scientists were keen to stress that such a pandemic was still *overdue*. The episode had seen a flurry of references to previous deadly viruses, especially the Spanish flu of 1918 and the Hong Kong flu of 1968. "Health experts said it was only a matter of time before a powerful new bug emerged to cause a pandemic, after a 35-year gap since the last one," one British newspaper reported.[94]

AVIAN FLU

FLU WAS INDEED TO PROVIDE the next of the scares that briefly gripped financial markets; namely bird flu. Cases of bird flu – or avian influenza – were already in evidence in Asia at around the same time as the SARS outbreak. This particular strain of flu continued to spread through Asia in 2004, although its impact was almost entirely limited to birds at this point, hurting poultry farmers in particular, but also the wider food trade. Nevertheless, some experts had already begun preparing the public for the worst.

"The world is teetering on the edge of a pandemic that could kill a large fraction of the human population," wrote Robert G. Webster in the March-April 2003 edition of *American Scientist*. Professor Webster – a leading virologist – went on to invoke the Spanish flu that killed between 20 and 40 million in the aftermath of the First World War. "Many epidemiologists believe a similar scenario will happen again. But this time will be worse." The nightmare scenario that scientists outlined was if the bird flu virus mutated such that it could be passed directly between humans. While humans were becoming infected and even dying from it, these were typically people who were living at close quarters with poultry.

By early November 2005, avian influenza was estimated to have killed more than 60 people over the previous three years, more than half of whom lived in Vietnam.[95] Although this death-toll was utterly unexceptional, the dread was beginning to spread among investors.

Economists at the Asian Development Bank – a multinational body working to eliminate poverty across the region – suggested that a full-blown bird flu epidemic could cost Asia alone millions of lives and some $250bn in lost economic growth.[96] With infected birds making their way beyond Asia, predictions of impending doom were heard in some faraway places. One of the starkest warnings of all came from BMO Nesbitt Burns, a well-known brokerage house in Canada.

In a report published in August 2005, Sherry Cooper, BMO Nesbitt Burns's chief economist, warned that the effects of an avian influenza pandemic could be similar to those of the Great Depression of the 1930s. Among the likely consequences was a collapse of real estate prices, soaring bankruptcies and decimation of the insurance industry. "We won't have 30-per-cent unemployment because frankly, many people will die," said Ms Cooper. "And there will be excess demand for labour and yet, at the same time, it will absolutely crunch the economy worldwide."[97]

BDO Nesbitt Burns's analysis received some endorsement from the scientific world. Michael Osterholm, director of the Center for Infectious Disease Research and Policy at the University of Minnesota, said that the financial industry was finally waking up to the dangers a pandemic posed to the economy and that an unprecedented collapse of international trade might be in store. "All the other catastrophes we've had in the world in recent years at the very most put screen doors on our borders. This would seal shut a six-inch steel door," he added.[98]

The media's interest in avian influenza surged dramatically as cases of bird deaths were reported further and further away from Asia and into Europe, including Romania and Croatia. The number of references appearing in English news sources went up five-fold between August and October 2005. While this proved to be the height of the frenzy in the press, there was a further flurry of stories in the first quarter of 2006, as infected dead fowl were found in France, Greece and Italy. Chart 7.3 illustrates the reference to the subject in the press.

CHART 7.3 – AVIAN INFLUENZA REFERENCES IN THE PRESS

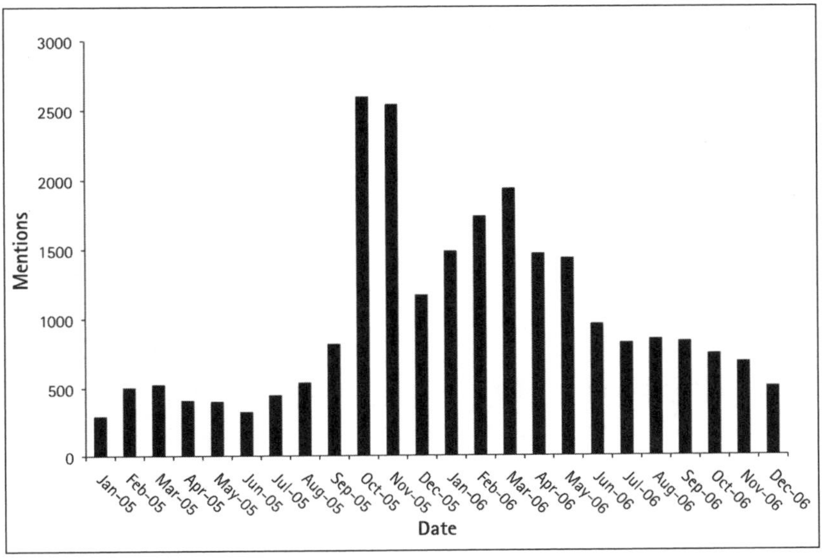

Source: Factiva

REFUGE SOUGHT IN PHARMACEUTICALS

Once again, the fear of a pandemic prompted investors to buy pharmaceutical stocks. The prime candidate was Roche, the Swiss maker of Tamiflu, an antiviral product that governments were stockpiling in case of a full-scale crisis. Roche's share price climbed 15 per cent in the three months to 13 October, almost double the gain in the Swiss Market Index during the same period. Biota – an Australian biotechnology company and producer of a rival anti-flu inhibitor – saw its share price quadruple over the same period.[99]

A rather more bizarre winner at the height of the bird flu scare was Pulmuone Co., South Korea's leading maker of health foods, including kimchi, the national dish. A rumour was rife in South Korea that kimchi – a pungent concoction of seasoned vegetables – could protect one from catching the disease. Following a weekend of worrisome news reports about the virus' progress, Pulmuone's share price jumped by ten per cent. Oddly enough, kimchi's prophylactic properties had also been touted during the SARS outbreak, causing Pulmuone's sales of this dish to rise by almost one-half.[100]

While cases of bird flu – both in fowl and in humans – continued to come to light in 2006 and 2007, the media and financial markets had refocused elsewhere. A new crisis erupted in the summer of 2007, which soon came to be known as the *credit crunch*.

THE CREDIT CRUNCH AND ECONOMIC CRISIS

THE BURSTING OF THE US HOUSING bubble brought to light vast amounts of grotesquely irresponsible lending and the questionable worth of mortgage-backed securities in particular. Credit markets around the world began to seize up as liquidity drained away.

COMPARISONS WITH THE GREAT DEPRESSION

The credit crunch and the economic deterioration that accompanied it were very serious problems indeed. The collapse in industrial production around the world was similar in its extent to that experienced at the start of the Great Depression in 1929-1930.[101] Stock markets and international trade initially suffered to an even worse degree than they had done during that earlier slump. National economies shrank at an alarming rate, while deflation made its first appearance for decades across many developed and emerging economies.

There was a genuine risk that the situation could have become even more dire than it did. Even as of early 2012, the crisis has not been definitively resolved, rather it has simply changed shape.

Governments' efforts to prevent a deep depression have left many of them groaning under the weight of enormous debts, which could result in their becoming insolvent in the coming years.

Despite the very real nature of the financial and economic crisis, many investors may have been overly seduced by the comparisons with the Great Depression of the 1930s. The media was once again instrumental in playing up this theme. Mentions of the Great Depression in the Anglophone press around the world in the six months before the credit crunch first struck averaged around 900 a month. This figure spiked to 7,540 in October 2008, the month after the collapse of Lehman Brothers. It remained elevated at above 3,000 a month for virtually the whole of 2009.

What was totally different about the economic crisis of 2008 and 2009 was the prompt response from governments and central banks around the world. Whereas the authorities in the 1930s generally kept interest rates high and tried to balance their budgets, their latter-day successors did the reverse. The scale of the response in the developed world was enough to produce an enormous rally in stocks, commodities and riskier bonds beginning in early 2009, which has stretched into 2012.

Despite the terrific gains in recent years, the fear of a depression has clearly continued to exert a hold over many investors, but particularly over private investors. Press references to the Great Depression have continued to figure at levels three times their pre-crisis average. Especially in cyberspace, there is a strong sense that large numbers of people are merely waiting for a financial apocalypse to take place.

INVESTORS SHUN STOCKS

The practical effect of this fear has been to keep many investors away from risky assets altogether. A noticeable feature of the rally in equities in countries including the US and the UK has been the shrinking number of shares changing hands. Volumes on the stock exchanges of New York and London have fallen persistently since early 2009, which is an unprecedented happening in the history of bull markets. One reason for this could well be that many investors do not believe in the recovery in the economy or in equities.

This notion is supported by the proportion of assets held by investors in US mutual funds. Despite the improvement in the US stock market – with the S&P 500 index having more than doubled in the three years to March 2012 – investors continued to hold vast amounts in bond mutual funds compared to their holdings of equity mutual funds. Traditionally, investors have shifted away from fixed-income investments and towards the stock market once a revival is underway.

Investing heavily in bonds – or at least in the highest-quality bonds – was a good strategy during the Great Depression of the 1930s and it has served investors well during Japan's multi-decade slump since 1989. It is also an understandable response of people who have been exposed to a string of traumas and scares, beginning with 9/11. Put simply, many investors and commentators seem nowadays to live in fear of the next terrible event, be it a meltdown of the eurozone, a crash in the US dollar, or a 1970s-style oil-price shock.

THE LESSONS OF THESE EPISODES

THIS CONSTANT FOCUS ON DRAMATIC, newsworthy risks is an example of what the school of behavioural finance calls the *availability heuristic*. When we try and assess the probability of something, we use certain mental short-cuts in order to do so. Our judgement is subconsciously influenced by facts that come most readily to mind. Prominent events that have appeared in the media – terrorist attacks, diseases, prognostications of economic collapse – are things we are especially likely to seize upon in this process.

As we have seen, focusing on sensational risks can deter us from making perfectly viable investments that are actually in our interests. It can also distract us from other less eye-catching – but perhaps much more relevant – risks. For example, seeking refuge in government bonds today because one is terrified of some extreme event ignores the risk of seeing one's investment gradually lose its value over time from the inflation that the authorities are deliberately but silently creating.

If the contemporary fashion for constantly obsessing over apocalyptic outcomes is irrational, logic says that it could also present an investment opportunity. The 19th century financier Baron Rothschild famously once remarked that the "time to buy is when there is blood running in the streets." This could well extend to episodes when there is merely the phantom menace of a bloody outcome, be it one caused by some pandemic, a terrorist atrocity or whatever the scare of the day happens to be.

In all the cases touched upon in this chapter, the existing trend in the stock market prevailed. While investors may have initially scrambled to buy into arms-makers and pharmaceutical firms, or sold airlines and hoteliers, the effects were almost invariably short-lived. Prior to 9/11, the US stock market was already in decline and it continued falling for more than a year thereafter. When the bird flu scare struck, the trend was manifestly upwards and the market continued to drive relentlessly higher.

The best approach in these situations was therefore to ignore the hysteria and concentrate on the stock market's prevailing trend. A simple way of establishing the market's trend is to observe whether the index's price is above or below its 200-day moving average, and whether that average is itself rising or falling. When the price is above its rising moving average, it can be said to be in an uptrend, for example. In the months before 9/11, the S&P 500 had been consistently below its 200-day average, which was also declining.

Chart 7.4 shows the S&P 500 from January 1997 to September 2002, with the 200-day moving average superimposed.

CHART 7.4 – TREND-SPOTTING IN THE S&P 500

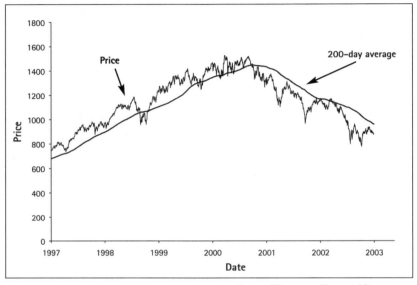

Source: Thompson Financial Datastream

Of course, it is always easy to speak with great wisdom about past episodes of irrational fear. In doing so, there is a danger of becoming complacent about future scares. One day, there may indeed be a global pandemic that is more devastating than the Spanish flu of 1918, or a terrorist attack even more spectacular than 9/11. Acknowledging such risks, however, is not the same thing as allowing one's entire mentality and investment strategy to be influenced by them. Obsessing over the next catastrophe is good for selling newspapers, but it is a formula for missing opportunities in the markets.

ENDNOTES

[79] 'Many Americans Stressed on 9/11, Even Though They Were Not There', Mental Health News Today, (21 September 2011); and 'The September 11, 2001 Terrorist Attacks: Ten Years After', *Journal of Traumatic Stress* 24:5 (October 2011), pp. 495-613.

[80] Diagnosis of PTSD – Persistent avoidance and emotional numbing (**www.supportforptsd.com/PTSDDiagnosis.aspx**).

[81] Estimates from Costs of War (**www.costsofwar.org**).

[82] 'Progress in the War on Terrorist Financing', The Investigative Project on Terrorism (11 September 2003), **www.investigativeproject.org/documents/testimony/60.pdf**

[83] Christopher Booker and Richard North, *Scared to death: From BSE to Global Warming – Why Scares Are Costing the Earth* (Continuum UK, 2007), pp.164-166.

[84] Clive Cookson, 'Health bodies warn on danger of germ warfare', *Financial Times* (26 September 2011).

[85] Rick Weiss, 'Bioterrorism: An Even More Devastating Threat', *Washington Post* (17 September 2001).

[86] Julian Borger, 'Cropdusters grounded in poison alert', *Guardian* (24 September 2011).

[87] John J. Fialka, Marilyn Chase, Neil King, Jr., and Ron Winslow, 'Attack On America: Chemical, Biological Threat Looms Larger for U.S.', *Wall Street Journal Europe* (19 September 2001).

[88] Professor Andrew Burd, 'An invisible killer in our midst', BBC (14 March 2003).

[89] Simon Benson and Anna Patty, 'Worse than Aids', *The Daily Telegraph* (25 April 2003).

[90] 'Estimates of Deaths Associated with Seasonal Influenza, United States, 1976-2007', Centers for Disease Control and Prevention (**www.cdc.gov/mmwr/preview/mmwrhtml/mm5933a1.htm**).

[91] Michael Morgan and Chris Flood, 'SARS sends Asian economies into downward spiral', *Financial Times* (25 April 2003).

[92] 'Battling SARS: Top Economist Expects Global Recession', *Wall Street Journal Asia*; and 'Morgan Stanley's Roach Calls Deadly Pneumonia "Another Nail in the Coffin"', Capital Markets Asia (4 April 2003).

[93] References to Severe Acute Respiratory Syndrome (SARS), all publications in English.

[94] 'Global killers – Invisible threat of mutant bugs', *The Scotsman* (17 March 2003).

[95] Luz Baguioro, 'Singapore, HK worst hit if bird flu spreads', *The Straits Times* (4 November 2005).

[96] David Lague, 'Asian bank sees huge flu impact on economy', *International Herald Tribune* (26 October 2005).

[97] 'Flu pandemic could trigger a Depression', *The Toronto Star* (17 August 2005).

[98] 'Flu pandemic could trigger a Depression', *The Toronto Star* (17 August 2005).

[99] Nicholas Zamiska, 'Flu Scare Leads Investors to Bet On Small Firms', *Wall Street Journal Europe* (13 October 2005).

[100] Zamiska, 'Flu Scare'.

[101] Miguel Almunia, Agustín S. Bénétrix, Barry Eichengreen, Kevin H. O'Rourke and Gisela Rua, 'From Great Depression to Great Credit Crisis: Similarities, Differences and Lessons', *Economic Policy* 25:62, pp. 221-265 (April 2010).

CHAPTER 8

WHEN RULES AND REGULATORS FAIL

THERE COULD HARDLY HAVE been a more trusted body than the Equitable Life Assurance Society. The world's first mutually-owned life insurer was founded in London in 1762, and pioneered the business of accepting premiums from policyholders and paying out guaranteed sums to their heirs upon death. Based on mortality tables developed by Edmund Halley – of comet fame – Equitable Life's scientific approach to insuring against the inevitable laid the foundations for the life insurance industry as we know it today.

Almost two-and-a-half centuries after its creation, however, Equitable Life was ignominiously forced to close its doors to new business. In 2000, it was revealed that this venerable organisation had made irreconcilable promises to its various groups of policyholders and did not have sufficient risk capital to bridge the gap. This was a complete disaster for Equitable's more than one million policyholders – mainly middle-class professionals – many of whom were depending on it for their retirement income.[102]

Equitable itself was aware from as early as the 1980s that it was heading for trouble. However, nobody informed the industry's regulators of the risks, nor did those regulators appear to look. The difficulties became public in 1993 and Equitable took to robbing

Peter to pay Paul in order to meet its profit-bonus commitments. Yet the regulators still showed scant interest.

It was only some five years later in 1998 that a drift of complaints to the Personal Investment Authority prompted the regulator to take legal steps towards a declaration of the competing rights of two different sorts of policyholders: those with *guaranteed annuities*, which Equitable Life didn't have the funds to honour, and the *current annuity holders*, whose non-guaranteed returns Equitable Life had effectively raided to make up the shortfall.

After a tortuous succession of hearings, the case came before the House of Lords, the highest court in the UK. In July 2000, it was ruled that Equitable must uphold its guarantee. This verdict was of little practical significance, however, as the necessary money wasn't there. Soon afterwards, Equitable Life was largely dismembered and sold, such that by 2008, its assets stood at just a quarter of their value eight years earlier.[103] Most importantly, nearly a million policyholders were £4.8 billion poorer than they would have been had they held properly-managed policies with one of Equitable's rivals.[104]

The case of Equitable Life encapsulates much of what is wrong with both regulations and regulators. A predictable flurry of government reports followed Equitable's undoing, jabbing the finger of blame in every direction. But this was all too late to help the policyholders who had suffered such heavy losses. Rather than intervening as doctors would do when faced with a sick patient, the regulators merely played the part of financial pathologists, carrying out a thorough and very public post mortem. The Equitable case is far from isolated; in numerous other cases, regulators have only reacted long after the fact.

In this chapter we will look at examples of failures by regulators, and the accounting and legal bodies that are supposed to police business' financial operations, and ask ourselves why these failures occur.

Regulators and their regulations

The ineffectiveness of regulations and regulators extends well beyond the United Kingdom. One might imagine that the United States would do a better job. After all, the US has a reputation for taking corporate wrongdoing seriously and boasts some well-established and weighty public watchdogs, such as the Securities and Exchange Commission (SEC) and the Department of Justice (DoJ). These institutions are decently resourced and have a predilection for cunning methods, such as wire-taps and bugging. Surely these US regulators must do a better job of heading off problems at an early stage?

The case of Bernie Madoff pours cold water on any such notion.

Madoff's Ponzi scheme

Bernie Madoff was responsible for history's biggest ever Ponzi scheme, a variation on a pyramid scheme, where the money new investors put into a fund is paid out to existing investors. He operated his ultimately-bogus investment funds for some three decades, largely unhindered by Wall Street's regulators.[105] Granted, the suspiciously high and improbably consistent returns that Madoff purported to be achieving did result in his being brought to the attention of the regulators – no less than eight times over 16 years – but nothing came of these probes. Madoff's fraud persisted and assumed epic proportions.

There was a suspicion that Madoff was engaging in front-running, buying a security for his firm's own account ahead of executing the same trade on behalf of a client. An SEC probe in 2004 found no evidence of this, however. The following year, the SEC examined his trades again, sampling a series of deals over a four-day period. Once more, it concluded that Madoff was following the strategy that he claimed to be.[106] The SEC appears to have looked at the paperwork relating to the transactions, though not necessarily the corresponding bank statements, which would have been harder to falsify.

FANTASY RETURNS

What makes the SEC's failure to spot wrongdoing in this case so inexcusable is that it had already long since received outright and detailed allegations that Madoff was running a Ponzi scheme. In 1999, Harry Markopolous, a securities analyst at an options-trading house, had examined Madoff's strategy and its purported returns with a view to trying to replicate them. He quickly found that both were impossible. Carrying out the strategy would have required Madoff to purchase more traded options than actually existed on the Chicago Board Options Exchange (CBOE). Markopolous made a series of direct representations to the SEC, culminating in a 21-page report in late 2005 that was none-too-subtly entitled 'The World's Largest Hedge Fund is a Fraud'.[107]

One defence that the regulators might offer for such failings as these is that they are overburdened with their caseload. Trawling through documents and looking for infringements of specific laws is a time-consuming business. However, Harry Markopolous was able to rumble Madoff's fraud on his own, with his initial suspicions aroused in some five minutes and then confirmed after four hours of financial modelling. Mr Markopolous took a step back and looked at the bigger picture, and then asked some simple but highly pertinent questions.

The lesson from the Madoff case and from many of the other biggest financial disasters of recent times is that the devil isn't so much lurking in the detail, but living brazenly in broad daylight. The fundamental flaws are there for all to see, if only the time is taken to scrutinise them. Madoff was claiming to achieve eye-catching returns that were mathematically implausible; Equitable

Life was plainly promising hundreds of thousands of policyholders money that it did not have.

ALLEGED FIXING OF THE LIBOR MARKET

A recent example of how regulators can miss the wood for the trees arose in the alleged fixing of the LIBOR market.[108] The London Inter-bank Offered Rate (LIBOR) is probably the most important benchmark in the world's money markets. LIBOR rates measure the cost that banks pay to borrow from one other. Their level therefore helps determine the calculation of countless other interest rates, from those paid by individuals to those for giant corporations. Some $6 trillion of financial contracts were linked to LIBOR at the time of writing.[109]

On the face of it, there is little real prospect of tampering with LIBOR. To do so would mean somehow influencing a fair few of the dozens of brokers who submit their offered rates to a panel, from which the outlier figures are removed by Thomson-Reuters. The news agency then calculates the average rate on behalf of the British Bankers Association. While manipulating this would be hard, however, there is an obvious motive to try to affect the rate, even if only for a short period.

Imagine the case of a large company or financial institution that has taken a loan at a floating rate of interest from a bank. However, it would prefer to pay a fixed rate of interest, and therefore know exactly what it will have to pay to service its debt going forward. So, it enters into a swap agreement, transforming its floating-rate liability into a fixed-rate one. The lower LIBOR is at the moment it enters this agreement, the lower its borrowing costs will be, potentially saving hundreds of millions over the life of the entire loan in the case of very big loans.

Trouble in the world of LIBOR was first suspected during the banking crisis of 2008. Despite a big increase in market measures of risk, the benchmark LIBOR rates failed to move upwards. A subsequently-published academic study has found that banks' own estimates of borrowing costs were surprisingly closely bunched together given that they faced very different levels of risk.[110] Once again, the fact that this has taken the best part of four years to reach the attention of regulators shows that some things might just be too big to see.

THE REASONS BEHIND REGULATORY FAILURES

So, why have regulators so often been ineffective just when they were needed most? In broad terms, they often are more concerned with processes than with outcomes. They pay great attention to less significant matters and fail to get to grips with the underlying risks. It appears that at times they fail to see the bigger picture.

For instance, while Bernie Madoff was running his Ponzi scheme, the SEC was busily engaged in investigating whether he was in fact operating an investment advisory business instead of running funds. Rather than getting a percentage of profits on his funds, Madoff appeared to be receiving commissions, which would have been a breach of regulations, albeit a far lesser one than his egregious fraud. In response, he merely adjusted the way he cooked his books in order to deflect the regulators' quibbles and then carried on fleecing his overly trusting clients of multiple millions.

While it is true that big fish can occasionally be caught on small hooks, the SEC's efforts were a distraction. If regulators were empowered to model the workings of firms, in the same way as investment analysts like Markopolos did, they might stand a chance of differentiating between minor infractions and the really serious and damaging ones. This is not to say that modelling is a failsafe approach in these cases, but it can be of use.

Another issue is that as civil servants, regulators often do not fully appreciate the workings of the commercial entities that they are charged with overseeing. Compared to the salaries paid by those commercial entities, the remuneration for regulators is often modest, resulting in an imbalance of talent between the overseers and the overseen. Those with the best modelling and analytical skills are most likely to be lured into the higher-paying private sector, rather than into a more modestly rewarded career as a watchdog.

The form that regulations take

United States

Despite the shortcomings of regulations – and of those who enforce them – there are examples of successful regulation. Certain provisions of the US Banking Act of 1933 – often called the Glass-Steagall Act – introduced deposit insurance for banks' customers, restricted interstate banking, and separated commercial banking and securities firms. The benefits of this act were enjoyed for two generations, before what was left of the law was finally repealed in 1999. It prevented banks from growing to a size where they became *too big to fail* and it helped to protect depositors when banks did go under.

Of the same stripe as the Glass-Steagall provisions is the Volcker rule, part of the Dodd-Franks Act that came into effect in 2010, which bans US banks from trading for speculative purposes on their own account.[111] It is rather a blunt instrument, as was Glass-Steagall. For example, a bank dealing for its own account in US Treasury securities probably poses fewer risks both to its own capital and to the wider financial system than if the same bank were to deal in highly leveraged derivatives on behalf of a large foreign client. The Volcker rule prevents the former, though, and does not affect the latter.

While the Volcker rule itself appears to be an effective idea, both it and the wider act of which it is part surely qualify as some of the most labyrinthine set of rules ever created. The Volcker rule originally ran to 11 pages. However, after four regulatory agencies became involved, it ballooned into a 298-page monster of a document. According to Davis Polk, a law firm representing some of the financial organisations to which the rules apply, this one small part of the Dodds-Frank Act potentially involves answering up to 383 questions and 1,420 sub-questions.[112]

The same regulators were responsible for the transformation of a two-page section dealing with hedge funds into a 192-page form, which some hedge funds reckon might cost $100,000 or so to fill out.[113] The entire act, at 848 close-typed pages, is ten times the size of Glass-Steagall. Unlike its 1930s predecessor, though, this act is really more of a template for regulators to create additional rules than an actual list of rules. In the style of the sorcerer's apprentice, it can therefore keep expanding, with over-the-counter transactions its next target, as of the time of writing. Davis Polk's own summary for clients, available on its website, runs to 130 pages.[114]

The underlying issue here is not merely the cost of compliance, but about the obfuscation of underlying principles. Simply because of its sheer size, no key financial decision-maker is ever likely to read the act. Even compliance officers will probably rely on summaries handed out by their lawyers, of which in turn only a handful will have really studied it. Such a complex piece of rule-making is unlikely to achieve anything other than making financial organisations constantly nervous that they may unwittingly be somehow in breach. This merely serves to enrich lawyers at the expense of banks, financial firms and, ultimately, their customers.

BRITAIN

Britain has a similarly unfortunate propensity towards churning out convoluted legislation. The Financial Services Authority (FSA), which regulates almost all of Britain's financial services industry, inevitably added to its rules after the banking crisis of 2007-2008. Law and accountancy firms were said to have been relieved that these additions amounted to only a six per cent growth in the FSA's 2009 handbook, the industry's regulatory bible. In absolute terms, though, it was a substantial increase of 497 pages.[115] The previous year the handbook had already swelled by an additional 2,000 pages.

REGULATION FROM THE EU

Locally-created rules are only part of the story in Britain and in every other country that belongs to the European Union. There are also the overarching financial regulations that Brussels imposes, each of which must be enshrined into national law and reconciled with the existing rules.

Not only can supra-national regulation be more complicated, it is more politicised because officials from individual member states typically have an underlying national agenda. The original aims are often commendable. The Undertakings for Collective Investment in Transferable Securities (UCITS) is an EU-wide rule first enacted in 1985, whose aim was to allow securities held by open-ended funds to be traded under a single set of rules across the entire EU. Today, this makes life easier when trading assets whose total value runs to several trillion dollars[116] but there is added complication in that individual member states have bolted on myriad rules to the original UCITS framework.

Nevertheless, UCITS remains a success story in the realm of supra-national regulation, albeit one of very few. Economic and political rivalries between European countries may have been somewhat suppressed following the formation of the EU, but they certainly have not disappeared altogether. Nowadays, these rivalries manifest themselves in more subtle ways, such as in the creation of regulations, one example being the attempts, led by France, to impose further strictures on the continent's banking system, and another being the German-inspired programme of instilling fiscal discipline into national governments.

Britain's Prime Minister, David Cameron, has regularly clashed with his European counterparts over attempts to impose a Europe-wide financial transaction tax, less onerous bank capital requirements across Europe than Britain wants domestically and to move the European Banking Authority away from London.[117] While Britain does not use the single European currency itself, more than half of the City of London's business takes place with those that do. The EU's proposed rule-changes threaten to affect not only UK-owned banks but also the London-based subsidiaries of American institutions, even for deals occurring entirely between non-eurozone parties. Mr Cameron and many others believe the changes could crimp the City of London's competitiveness, making it more expensive to do business there and resulting in a loss of business to Asian and US financial centres.

ENFORCEMENT OF REGULATION

The details of regulation alone do not determine its effectiveness. Enforcement is another vital element. It has long been noted that the US imposes much more severe penalties on most forms of regulatory breach than other countries around the world. Long prison sentences are handed down in cases that might not even attract any jail-time at all elsewhere. This creates an especially sharp contrast with Japan, which has a history of failing to enforce regulations in a deterrent fashion.

Until March 2012, for example, no bank had ever been fined in Japan for insider dealing, despite the suspicion that this illicit activity is rampant in the land of the rising sun. Chuo Mitsui Asset Trust (CMAT) has since been fined for its involvement in a long-running string of insider deals, in which a fund manager at CMAT was given privileged inside information by an employee of a bank that was working on a forthcoming issuance of equity for Impex, an oil developer, before the issue was announced.

Japan's Securities and Exchange Surveillance Commission spent more than a year investigating a series of allegations that insider activity lay behind price falls in a series of companies that were about to announce the issuance of new shares. Although this case was of landmark significance in Japanese financial markets, the regulator fined CMAT just ¥50,000 ($600). This sanction was clearly a flea-bite compared to the ¥14 million gain that CMAT had made on the insider deal. There was no penalty for the employee official at the underwriting bank who breached his regulatory duties by revealing the impending issue.[118]

EFFORTS BY FINANCIAL INSTITUTIONS TO SIDESTEP REGULATION

Disparities in regulation inevitably influence the decisions of financial institutions, not only in terms of where they domicile themselves, but also through which financial centres they channel business. They may face costly upheavals to move, but they can and certainly do make transactions and also hold funds in less heavily-regulated jurisdictions wherever possible. The temptations are just too great to do otherwise, as the behaviour of London-based hedge funds in the last five years has illustrated.

Hedge funds were dismayed by changes to UK's tax code some years ago, which shortened the amount of time a foreign individual could spend in the country without becoming liable to Britain's relatively high rates of personal income tax. The situation was exacerbated in 2010 by an increase in the top rate of income tax from 40 to 50 per cent. While these measures have not fatally undermined London's competitiveness, they encouraged a number of big-name hedge funds, including Brevan Howard and BlueCrest Capital, to move to Switzerland, where traders can benefit from personal income tax rates as low as ten per cent, more tranquil settings and greater proximity to the world's second biggest client pool.[119] At the same time, Switzerland was also moving to simplify some of its cantonal tax regulations to improve its overall tax competitiveness still further. As a result, one in four of London's hedge fund employees had moved to Switzerland by 2010.[120]

This massive relocation was predicated on the assumption that Switzerland would maintain its relaxed and light-touch regulatory regime. It therefore came as something of a shock to the hedge funds when in April 2012, the Swiss Federal Council proposed sweeping changes to the country's regulatory approach in an attempt to bring Switzerland into line with the EU's hedge-fund rules.

While these proposals are still only at the drafting stage – and indeed have not even been translated into English at the time of writing – they are said to be likely to include demands for asset and tax transparency, plus stipulations on governance and tough regulatory oversight.[121] The new rules may also strip wealthy individuals of their automatic *qualified investor* status, which allows them to pay money directly into hedge funds.[122] Whether the final rules turn out to be quite this draconian is hard to say, but it is clear that there are risks to hedge funds that tactically shift their domicile. Even Switzerland, it seems, cannot be trusted to keep itself on an even keel when it comes to regulation. For all that, capital has become ever more mobile, and onerous regulation – such as Dodd-Franks – only helps it to spur its movement.

LIGHT REGULATION IN SINGAPORE

While Switzerland could conceivably join London and New York in amassing a pile of regulations, Singapore has to date kept faith with the laissez-faire approach. This dates back to 1968, when the island republic, then a member of the sterling area, sought advice from Bank of America about how to establish a financial centre. Bank of America's straightforward advice was to set up an offshore eurodollar-type area such as Hong Kong had already done.

Despite opposition from the Bank of England, which wanted Singapore to retain exchange controls, Singapore's Prime Minister Lee Kuan Yew followed the advice. He exempted Asian deposits in US dollars from liquidity and reserve requirements, and left overseas interest income exempt from any withholding tax. Once the Bank of England relented and acceded to Singapore's move, business flourished. It was particularly buoyed by connections made outside Hong Kong's existing influence and by American spending in the region during the Vietnam War.

After the 1997 emerging-markets crisis, Singapore went further still. Buoyed by its survival of the crisis, it further lightened its regulatory touch, while also retaining strict banking secrecy.[123] A free-market think tank voted Singapore the second-most free economy in the world in 2011, after Hong Kong.[124] None of this is to say that Singapore's approach makes the global financial world any safer. The lack of transparency and light-touch regulation does not make it any easier to see or protect against frauds, bubbles or dangerous lending practices. However, the stark contrast with the bureaucratic swamp of Europe and North America will continue to make Singapore a haven for footloose wealth. And where the wealthy go, their bankers and associated service-providers must follow.

This principle extends to all kinds of lightly-regulated areas of finance. Over-the-counter (OTC) markets and offshore investments are all more lightly regulated than other more conventional markets. However, the regulators are again gradually closing in on these markets. By the third quarter of 2012 at the latest, the Dodd-Frank Act will cover any OTC transactions in which there is a US-based counterparty, and force clearance of those deals through a centralised counterparty. Similar measures are expected to be applied in Europe and Asia by the middle of next year,[125] and will for the first time force the use of collateral. While this will increase transparency and limit credit risk, it will certainly make OTC platforms much more expensive for those lacking suitable high-quality collateral.

The unintended consequences of regulation

Regulation and other official intervention almost always have unintended consequences. When regulators intervene they can create incentives that profit-seeking entities will find attractive. The Volcker rule forbidding speculative proprietary trading may well impel some institutions to create phoney offshore counterparties to act as a *client* in trades that are really for the institution's own account.

The Basel III rules on banks' capital adequacy inevitably lower banks' returns on capital by effectively keeping much of it available to sustain losses. These rules could tempt banks to try and pep up returns on their remaining capital by undertaking riskier activities than they otherwise would have done.

The government rescue of banks like Citibank and Bank of America that were deemed too big to be allowed to go under during the crisis of 2008 has given them an unfair advantage over institutions that are not deemed too big to fail. As Sheila Bair, then head of the Federal Deposit Insurance Corporation, said in an interview in October 2009:

> " 'Too big to fail' has become worse. It's become explicit when it was implicit before. It creates competitive disparities between large and small institutions, because everybody knows small institutions can fail. So it's more expensive for them to raise capital and secure funding."[126]

Already in 2009, a hundred small banks had failed. Most of these had only a minor role, if any, in the global financial crisis, but they just could not compete with the state-backed players who were the beneficiaries of bailout support. Bad practice, through capital costs, was driving out good. This is one of the lessons of well-intentioned regulatory efforts when those efforts are poorly thought through.

Accounting and legal bodies

Enron

REGULATION IS NOT SIMPLY about governments, though. It also concerns the accounting and legal bodies through which corporations present themselves to the outside world of investors, government agencies and customers. In terms of accounting, all companies are required to have independent professionals sign off their accounts as giving a fair and accurate view of their business, assets and liabilities. Any implicit faith that existed in such endorsements suffered a mortal blow in 2002, when the blue-chip auditing firm Arthur Andersen was convicted of obstruction of justice for shredding incriminating documents relating to its work with Enron, the disgraced energy trading firm.[127]

Enron was a company that fooled everyone. On the face of it, it was a model corporation. It was named *Fortune* magazine's 'most innovative company' for six years running and was on *Forbes* magazine's list of the top 100 companies to work for in America. Beneath its polished public image, however, the firm used accounting loopholes to hide debt in off-balance sheet vehicles and revenue was recognised in a very aggressive way. Collectively, these complex machinations amounted to systematic and widespread accounting fraud, and when the company went bankrupt in December 2001 its $63 billion balance sheet made it at the time the largest corporate collapse in history.[128]

More painfully, many of Enron's 20,000 employees lost not only their jobs, but also their pensions and savings, much of which had again been tied up in the corporation's stock. Kenneth Lay, Enron's chairman, had continued to urge staff to buy stock in the firm in the months leading up to its collapse, even as he himself sold $16.3 million of shares. It might seem that Enron had either fooled or colluded with its own auditors[129] and that there was not much chance of any regulator catching on to what the company was up to. However, the clues of aggressive accounting policies were there for others to see. Enron had already gained permission from the SEC to use mark-to-market accounting for its natural gas operations, which allowed it to benefit from price rises in this commodity.

Enron used a so-called *merchant model* in its energy trading business, in which the value of contracts it dealt in were treated as revenue, rather than just the brokerage fee it earned on those contracts, which was the conventional model for that industry. Enron was thereby earning additional revenues as the energy contracts' value increased, but laying itself open to trouble if prices were ever to fall significantly. As a result, Enron managed to turn revenues of $13 billion in 1996 into $101 billion by 2000. Just as in the Madoff case, someone from among the many auditors, securities analysts, and regulators should have asked how on earth Enron had managed that, and whether it was sustainable and legal. Nobody did, however. In the same way that bad rules always drive out good, rivals like Duke Energy, Dynegy and reliant Energy also switched to merchant-type accounting, allowing them to build revenues fast enough to join Enron in the Fortune 500.[130]

It was a journalist, rather than a regulator or analyst, who finally asked some of the awkward questions that set Enron's decline in motion. In March 2001, Bethany McLean wrote an article in *Forbes* that pointed out the opacity of the company's financial statements and the lack of understanding of its business model among investors. As Enron's stock price slid alongside the wider US stock market during 2001, its chief executive Jeffrey Skilling mysteriously resigned in August, after just six months in his post. The stock then collapsed 14 per cent in just two days. Finally, Enron admitted inflating profits in November, and filed for bankruptcy the following month.

GREECE'S COVER-UP

When a sovereign nation cheats, the entire ethos of regulation is called into question. In 2001, Greece was struggling to meet the rules for joining the single European currency. Among other things, these demanded that Greece's national debt-load should be falling. This was not the reality, however, so Greek officials turned to Goldman Sachs. The investment bank proceeded to concoct a deal involving a €2.8 billion currency-swap arrangement at a fictitious exchange rate, such that Greece's debts appeared smaller than they were in reality.[131] The cost of this deal was originally €791 million, but bungled Greek attempts to cover this up by using interest rate derivatives served to inflate the total amount owed, including the swap, to €5.1 billion by 2005.[132] "The Goldman Sachs deal is a very sexy story between two sinners," said Christoforos Sardelis, who at the time was the head of Greece's debt management agency.[133]

The very notion that Greece was prepared to cook its books to gain access to the euro may seem shocking to some. In light of its subsequent failure to manage its excessive debts within a fixed exchange-rate regime, it also betrays a wilful disregard for the principles of economics, as well as of ethical conduct. Given that it occurred anyhow, presumably with the knowledge of those at the highest levels of government, how can the strictures of regulators in markets ever carry any weight?

Goldman Sachs said that the swap was only initiated when Greece had already entered the eurozone and that it had checked the transaction with Eurostat. The Brussels-based EU body, which sets accounting rules for national governments, retorted that it was never shown any details. According to Greek debt officials, the nature of the deal was well-known in the markets, raising the question of why Eurostat failed to notice that it was being sold a pup. Whatever the reason, the fact remains that an entire economy falsified its national accounts with the connivance of senior public officials and European Union-level regulators did not apparently notice. A decade later, the entire European economy is living with the costs of this failure. The total amount of eurozone taxpayers' money riding on that regulatory error, so far, is €130 billion; more than forty times the amount hidden by Greece.

CAVEAT EMPTOR

THE IMPULSE TO REGULATE is a natural one for governments. In many cases, the original motives are laudable. These include the detection, prevention and eradication of fraud, the protection of consumers, safeguarding the functioning of key financial sectors, and achieving a level commercial playing field. However, the means and processes by which legislators and regulators try to achieve its aims are flawed. Constructing and insisting upon compliance with intricate rules is no substitute for asking the right kind of questions. Investors cannot rely upon rules and regulators in this regard. *Caveat emptor* – let the buyer beware – is the first and best line of defence for those that regulation seeks to protect.

ENDNOTES

[102] 'Glick Report', joint opinion of Ian Glick QC and Richard Snowden for the Financial Services Authority (May 2001).

[103] Equitable Life, 2008 annual report.

[104] Sir John Chadwick, author of a report in 2008, quoted by BBC, 22 July 2010.

[105] Exactly when Madoff's empire began its slide into fraudulence is unknown, but it may have happened as early as the 1970s. It had definitely become fraudulent by the 1990s.

[106] *Wall Street Journal* (5 January 2009).

[107] 'The Man Who Figured Out Madoff's Scheme', CBS News (10 June 2009).

[108] At the time of writing, no charges have been pressed.

[109] *The Economist*, 14 April 2012.

[110] Rosa M. Abrantes-Metz, Michael Kraten, Albert D. Metz and Gim Seow, 'LIBOR Manipulation?' (4 August 2008).

[111] The Volcker rule is named after Paul Volcker, a former Chairman of the Federal Reserve, who was appointed to the President's Economic Recovery Advisory Board in February 2009.

[112] *The Economist* US edition (18 February 2012).

[113] *The Economist*, ibid.

[114] Davis Polk website (**www.davispolk.com**).

[115] BDO Stoy Hayward, quoted by John Bakie in IFA Online **www.ifaonline.co.uk/ifaonline/news/1352230/fsa-handbook-barely-grown-bdo**

[116] European Fund and Asset Management Association figures for 2008.

[117] In December 2011, Cameron and French President Nicolas Sarkozy held up a European summit by arguing into the small hours about the terms of EU financial regulation. Reported in the *Financial Times* (9 December 2011).

[118] *Financial Times* (27 March 2012), p. 19.

[119] *Financial Times* (7 September 2008).

[120] Estimate by consultancy Kinetic Partners, quoted in the *Financial Times* (1 October 2010).

[121] *Financial Times* (14 April 2012), p. 1.

[122] *Financial Times* (14 April 2012).

[123] Mapping Financial Secrecy, Tax Justice Network (October 2011).

[124] Fraser Institute of Canada.

[125] *Financial Times* (4 March 2012).

[126] *USA Today* (20 October 2009).

[127] The conviction was overturned by the Supreme Court in 2005 because of flaws in jury instruction.

[128] Original Texas state indictment (**news.findlaw.com/hdocs/docs/enron/usandersen030702ind.html**).

[129] Indictment, ibid.

[130] Bala G. Dharan and William R. Bufkins, 'Red Flags in Enron's Reporting of Revenues and Key Financial Measures', Social Science Research Network (July 2008), p. 105.

[131] Nick Dunbar, *Newsnight* (20 February 2012).

[132] *Newsnight*, ibid.

[133] Nick Dunbar, Bloomberg News (5 March 2012).

CHAPTER 9
THE MORAL HAZARD OF MONEY

LORD'S CRICKET GROUND in London is a bastion of English reserve. It came as something of a shock, therefore, when Allen Stanford, a Texan financier, landed in a helicopter at this genteel venue in June 2008 and paraded before spectators with a giant Perspex cube containing US$20 million in cash.[134] This princely sum was the prize in a new winner-takes-all cricket tournament that Stanford was promoting. While some welcomed this injection of razzmatazz and lucre into what has often been seen as a rather stuffy and underfunded sport, cricketing purists grumbled that no good could possibly come of it.

The purists turned out to be correct, albeit perhaps not for the reasons that they had initially suspected. Stanford was subsequently exposed as a fraudster, whose $7 billion Caribbean-based financial empire was no more than a giant Ponzi scam.[135] The munificent prize that Stanford was offering to the winning cricket team was quite simply not his money to give.

FINANCIAL FRAUDSTERS

ALLEN STANFORD'S FRAUD was merely the latest case in the long history of financial trickery. But while we now know the intimate details of what Stanford and his many infamous predecessors did, we have a much less clear idea of how these people think and what really motivates them. Self-enrichment may not be the sole force at work here, nor even the most important one in some cases. We also need a better understanding of the mentality both those who are supposed to spot financial fraudsters and yet fail to do so, and also what causes the fraudsters' victims to succumb.

The crimes of Allen Stanford and his ilk stand out not only because of their magnitude, but also because of their peculiar nature. A typical miscreant with any sense seeks to operate in the shadows and then to flee the scene of his crime promptly. By contrast, Stanford positively courted publicity and persisted with his fraud for as long as he possibly could. The physical trappings of his ill-gotten wealth were not enough for him. He craved a social status to match his super-sized riches and this may well have inspired his decision to base himself where he did.

The tiny island nations of Montserrat and Antigua offer the attractions of a tropical climate and of famously unobtrusive financial regulation. But these Caribbean paradises also gave Stanford the opportunity to lead the existence of a very big fish in a small pond. The increasingly wealthy magnate was feted in Antigua, where he was a major employer and investor. He regularly rubbed shoulders with Baldwin Spencer, the prime minister. In 2006, the grateful country conferred upon its adoptive son the title of 'Knight Commander of the Most Distinguished Order of the Nation', enabling him to style himself 'Sir Allen'.[136] This honour bestowed by the state bolstered his reputation and earned him greater trust from his victims.

While his financial empire was built on lies, the advantages that Sir Allen brought to Antigua were genuine enough, at least for a time. Aside from creating jobs, he was a prominent benefactor to various local charities, and also sponsored cultural and sporting activities on the island. He made warm public proclamations, such as that of his "love for the Caribbean, its people and its future". But all this was not enough to shield him from his downfall. The Governor General of Antigua and Barbuda decided in 2009 that Sir Allen was to revert to being plain old Mr. Stanford even before he was convicted.[137]

FRAUDSTERS' SELF-JUSTIFICATION FOR THEIR ACTIONS

There would appear to be a fundamental contradiction in spending many years – as well as multiple millions – in building a reputation that one day faces spectacular destruction. One possibility is that the fraudster hopes that his past good works will serve to mitigate his crimes, if and when they are exposed. A more cynical explanation is that they may act as an effective disguise for his villainy. After all, someone who gives lavishly to good causes might logically be presumed to be a decent person and therefore less likely to engage in wrongdoing.

Of these two explanations, the use of philanthropy as a mask seems the more plausible. And, of course, giving some of the proceeds of crime to good causes does not alter the nature of those funds. It can even later prove to be to the detriment of the cause concerned. While Allen Stanford earned praise at the time for his gifts to St Jude's, a charity for children with cancer, that organisation was later sued by victims of his fraud in a bid to claw back some of that which he had stolen from them.

The other great Ponzi schemer of recent years also sought status through charitable activities. Bernie Madoff's $64 billion fraud was the largest in history. Along the way, he built up his own endowment fund of $19 million, which he used to donate to causes in his native New York, particularly those relating to the Jewish community from which he came.[138] Madoff's *mitzvah*s earned him much more than the admiration of his co-religionists, however; impressed by their benefactor's apparent genius for investment, many of the organisations to which he had given then entrusted him with managing their own endowment funds.

Charities were ideal victims for Madoff's Ponzi scheme. Their investment needs tend to be steady and predictable. In the US, charitable foundations are supposed to spend a fixed percentage of their funds each year on their stated cause and their running costs.[139] As a result, Madoff knew that they were unlikely suddenly to demand to withdraw large and unexpected sums that might jeopardise his crooked game. For instance, if a charity had given him $20 million to manage, he could simply pay them back $1 million a year out of their own funds. That gave him at least 20 years of breathing space and possibly more if he could continue pulling in new money from elsewhere.

Madoff's generosity towards Jewish charities enhanced his personal standing among this community more generally. In particular, it allowed him to circulate among members of the influential Modern Orthodox sect, despite not being orthodox himself. His enhanced status helped to attract billions of dollars worth of investments from wealthy individual Jews. Writing in the *New York Times*, Samuel G. Freedman explained how the nature of this community had left it open to abuse:

> "Their leaders and members overlap like a sequence of Venn diagrams. They are bound by religious praxis, social connection, philanthropic causes. Yet what may be the community's greatest virtue – its thick mesh of personal relations, its abundance of social capital – appears to have been the very trait that Mr. Madoff exploited."[140]

Madoff's quest for status extended well beyond New York's high society and Jewish circles. He and his wife made continual donations to the Democratic Party and also lobbied Congressmen, paying out a total of almost $1 million in the decade leading up to his exposure.[141] On more than one occasion, the political establishment returned the favour, even inviting him to testify as an expert witness before a Congressional committee on financial affairs. Without a doubt, the reputational gains he enjoyed from this made it easier for him to operate his giant scam.

As in the case of Allen Stanford, Madoff's painstakingly accumulated reputation was utterly obliterated when his Ponzi scheme collapsed in 2008. That he had defrauded charities and members of his own community actually left him more of a pariah than Stanford. Tova Mirvis, a Jewish author, summed up the feeling well:

> "If you wanted to write a novel about this, nobody would ever think it was plausible. It would feel unfathomable. For someone inside to do this to their own institutions? How? Why?"[142]

It is possible that neither Stanford nor Madoff thought they would ever be caught. Both would have realised that were they ever to be found out, the acceptance and respect they had built up would be instantly replaced by shame and loathing. But they may have begun to believe their own lies. Madoff had been swindling investors since the early 1990s and perhaps for many years before that, surviving eight investigations over 16 years by the Securities and Exchange Commission and other regulatory agencies.[143] By 2008 he was already 70 years old and might have reasonably expected to reach the end of his days before his wrongdoing caught up with him. Stanford, meanwhile, had successfully got away with his swindle for two decades.[144]

A Ponzi scheme is inevitably doomed to eventual failure. As a simple matter of arithmetic, the point is always reached where it becomes impossible to sucker in enough fresh investors to pay off the existing ones. As such, the ultimate disgrace of its perpetrator is also inevitable. By contrast, other varieties of financial fraudster have at least some chance of their misdeeds ending happily for them. One example of this is that of the rogue trader, of whom there seem to have been an increasing number of cases over the last few years, and to whom we shall return shortly.

How fraudsters escape notice

Having considered the motivations and mindset of those that commit financial fraud, we need also to address the thinking behind those who fall for it. Greed is often a driving force among these people. It is the unquenchable thirst for wealth that causes people to suspend their disbelief and accept at face value the fraudster's grandiose claims and promises of outsized and often risk-free returns.

Advance-fee fraud

Ordinary folk the world over fall victim to scams every day, but particularly in cyberspace. Perhaps the most notorious of these are *advance-fee* frauds. These begin with an email that typically offers the recipient a massive payment in return for their passive assistance in transferring loot amassed by a deceased African general or the inheritance of some Asian tycoon's widow that is currently stuck in an obscure location. All that is required to liberate these funds is for the recipient to allow them to be transferred to his or her bank account. In return, the dupe will receive a cut amounting to hundreds of thousands or even millions of dollars.

Naturally, the vast majority of those who receive these unsolicited emails despatch them summarily to their trash folder with a chuckle, but the occasional person who takes the bait is soon asked to contribute to various upfront costs associated with transferring the money, such as legal fees, telex charges, visa services and a whole litany of other spoof expenses. At the same time, the fraudster tries to keep the victim's attention fixed on the ultimate glittering prize. The latter pays out hundreds and then thousands, becoming ever more psychologically wedded to the desire to stay the course and secure the pot of gold at the end of the rainbow, despite his growing misgivings and losses.

The use of email makes this sound like a very modern scam. However, the pedigree of advance-fee fraud goes back very many years. In the 1920s American Midwest, a fraudster called Oscar Hartzell managed to defraud 70,000 ordinary families of a total of $2 million by telling them he had discovered they were descendents of the 16th century English admiral and explorer Sir Francis Drake.[145] Hartzell claimed that he was seeking to distribute Sir Francis' long-lost estate, which was valued in the hundreds of millions of dollars, to his rightful heirs. Many families lost their homes or farms after having mortgaged them trying to meet Hartzell's continuous demands for expenses.

FAILURE TO ASK THE RIGHT QUESTIONS

In a world of rational decision-makers, it would be much harder for people to fall for scams such as these. The reality, of course, is that the world is not made up of the calculating beings that the economic textbooks imply. Aside from our inability to process information efficiently, we seldom have all the necessary facts at our disposal. One party to a transaction typically knows something that the other doesn't, the classic example being that of the seller of a second-hand car with a hidden defect.[146] This asymmetry is especially severe when it comes to fraudulent propositions.

One solution to this problem of *asymmetric information* is to perform due diligence but it is clear that people do not always do this to anything like the extent that they should, especially where large amounts are at stake. In his seminal study of the famous 1990s Ponzi scheme of the Foundation for New Era Philanthropy, Professor Steven Pressman contends that it is not that investors try but fail to get the most information, but that they simply do not try at all:

> "...the problem is that investors themselves do not ask the appropriate questions and naïvely believe what they are told and apparently what they want to believe."[147]

New Era Philanthropy was a non-for-profit organisation ostensibly meant to help companies direct their philanthropic spending. John G. Bennett used this organisation's honourable purpose to defraud charities of many millions of dollars. Rather than promising access to some fantastic investment opportunity, he was dangling before them the best connections in the world of Christian philanthropy.

Bennett conned charities into letting him direct their investments and promised that he could double their funds in six months through getting other wealthy donors, who wanted to remain anonymous, to match their funding.[148] This would not normally have required the charities to lodge their money with him, but Bennett claimed he needed the interest from it to cover his expenses. When this Ponzi scheme came unstuck in May 1995, it owed $551 million and had just $80 million in assets.[149]

Faced with a complex decision involving uncertainty rather than a quantifiable risk, Pressman argues that investors look to a trusted focal point for more information. The first point of reference is often a friend or acquaintance who has already invested. With a sufficiently large number of such supportive referees, it is easy to create a herd instinct, which plays into the fraudster's hands. This is especially true when it comes to Ponzi and pyramid schemes, in which the early investors do actually get paid out with the promised returns, funded by the fresh subscriptions of newcomers to the scheme.

Why did charities – run by professionals and with investment experience aplenty – fail to do their homework properly here? According to Professor Pressman, the reasons are largely psychological. Individuals are by nature both optimistic and overly-confident in their own judgement. They are influenced by the halo effects of the context within which an investment is framed. A charitable organisation like New Era Philanthropy created the right conditions for acceptance within the Christian philanthropic community upon which it preyed. After all, Bennett appeared to be one of their own. At the same time, Bernie Madoff was using exactly the same approach within the most affluent circles of New York's Jewish community.

EXPERTS SUCCUMB TOO

It is perhaps not all that surprising that ordinary members of the public fall for Ponzi schemes, since they lack the time and expertise to dig deeper. But is rather puzzling how the smartest specialists, often veterans in their field, get suckered in by *too-good-to-be-true* marketing pitches. Bramdean Alternatives, an asset management firm run by Nicola Horlick, a star British fund manager, had £10m invested in Bernie Madoff's funds and she was stunned when it emerged that he was a con man. Just a few months before the Madoff Empire came crashing down, Ms Horlick gave a glowing endorsement of the fraudster-in-chief and his investment strategy:

> "He is someone who is very good at calling the US equity market... if he's really negative then he puts cash into US treasuries... if he's positive then he puts on a derivative trade... it's actually called a collar, which limits the upside, but also the downside... This guy has managed to return 1 to 1.2 per cent per month, year after year after year."[150]

Ms Horlick was not alone. Dozens of top professional fund managers were taken in on a grand scale. Among the blue-chip victims were Fairfield Greenwich Group, which had $7.5 billion invested in Madoff funds, Tremont Capital ($3.3 billion), Banco Santander ($2.87 billion), Banco Medici ($2.10 billion), Fortis ($1.35 billion) and HSBC ($1 billion).[151]

Madoff's advertised returns and consistency, which for one fund averaged 10.5 per cent annually over 17 years, were not impossible, but highly unlikely. Only a handful of investors have ever genuinely achieved such a track record, and none using the particular methods that Madoff claimed to employ. Aside from his consistently high returns, Madoff also seemed virtually immune to stock-market turmoil. In November 2008, at which point the S&P 500 was down 38 per cent for the year to date, one Madoff fund which concentrated on equities from that index was supposedly up by 5.6 per cent.[152] Only in one month in every 25 did Madoff funds report a fall, which should have raised eyebrows given the high-octane derivatives that he claimed to be using.

Not everyone was fooled. "It took me five minutes to know that it was a fraud," said Harry Markopolous, the financial analyst who reported Madoff to the Securities and Exchange Commission on five separate occasions. "It took me another almost four hours of mathematical modelling to prove that it was a fraud."[153] So, if a relatively obscure analyst like Markopolous had suspicions after five minutes, it is surprising that others didn't experience the same misgivings after the exhaustive due diligence that they claimed to have performed.

Exclusivity, trust and secrecy

Madoff used very much the same psychological ploys that both John G. Bennett and Oscar Hartzell had done. One of these was exclusivity. Direct contact with Madoff was meted out sparingly. To be granted an audience with him was a great honour. He would rarely meet even big investors directly and used a network of feeder funds to channel money in. He would rarely accept funds directly. This made investors fear that if they did withdraw any of their funds, they might not be able to get back in again later on[154], which was a master stroke of Madoff's indeed.

Creating an aura of trust is another essential element of Ponzi schemes. Madoff went about this in several ways. As we have seen, he was not only a big hitter in the philanthropic world, but also in Washington too. He had been on the board of the Securities Industry Association, which later became the Securities Industries and Financial Markets Association (SIFMA), the primary body representing the interest of the industry in Washington. Indeed, Peter Madoff, Bernie's brother, was on the board of SIFMA at the time of his undoing. The Madoff family gave more than $50,000 to SIFMA between 2000 and 2008, and spent thousands more sponsoring SIFMA events. The *New York Times* even reported that Arthur Levitt, who was SEC chief from 1993 to 2001, had occasionally asked Madoff's advice about the way markets worked, though he denied that Madoff exerted undue influence in the SEC or that Levitt's staff deferred to him. Still, with even regulators seeking his advice, Madoff clearly bore the imprimatur of the Washington insider as well as that of the Wall Street insider.[155]

A degree of secrecy is another further vital ingredient for the workings of Ponzi schemes, as the truth must be hidden from prying eyes. In Madoff's case, however, secrecy merely served to add a further level of mystique. Madoff didn't allow investors to access their accounts online. He rarely published insights into his trading methods, hinting that they were too sophisticated for ordinary investors to understand. The financial records of the firm were also a closely-guarded secret. But instead of raising suspicions, all this seemed to fit well with his image as an investor with the golden touch, who was understandably keen to keep his winning formula to himself.

ROGUE TRADERS

NICK LEESON AND BARINGS BANK

THE MODERN ERA OF ROGUE TRADING probably began with Nick Leeson, whose unauthorised activities brought his employer Barings Bank to its knees in 1995. Instead of pursuing the low-risk strategy of speculating on the relationship between various Japanese stock-market futures contracts as he was supposed to do, Leeson began making high-risk bets on the direction of the Japanese stock market. These went awry, however, and the losses began to stack up. Leeson managed to conceal his black hole and tried to refill it by placing ever larger bets, which also lost. His eventual losses of £827 million dwarfed Barings' capital and the blue-blooded British merchant bank was humiliatingly sold off for the sum of £1.

The Leeson affair is not an isolated one. The increasingly complicated world of financial derivative products has spawned a succession of lookalike cases, generally involving a trader losing vast sums by overreaching his authority and then masking his failures while trying desperately to break even by continuously doubling up his bets. Unlike the high-profile Ponzi schemers we have explored, these fraudsters have not sought fame and status, or at least not in the public eye. However, winning status in the eyes of one's employer may well play a part, with the hope of advancement and larger reward. The really interesting question is how much the employer is complicit within the process.

In the case of Barings, the bank's management was negligent and somewhat gullible. They had been forewarned that Leeson was of dubious character. In fact, they had dispatched him to work in their Singapore branch after he was denied a broker's licence in the UK owing to a fraudulent statement made on his application. Barings also allowed Leeson to act simultaneously as the head of trading and head of settlements, which gave him scope to camouflage his misdeeds for longer than he may otherwise have been able. The bank's culture also left it susceptible to trickery, as Leeson explains in his autobiography:

> "People at the London end of Barings were all so know-all that nobody dared ask a stupid question in case they looked silly in front of everyone else."[156]

Jérôme Kerviel and Société Générale

The banking industry really should have learned its lesson by the time that rogue trader Jérôme Kerviel lost his employer Société Générale €4.9 billion ($6.4 billion) in 2008. According to Société Générale (SG), Kerviel was also meant to be trying to exploit mispricings in equity-index derivatives. Like Leeson, he was initially accused of having "taken massive fraudulent directional positions in 2007 and 2008 far beyond his limited authority." The governor of the Banque de France, Christian Noyer, said at the time that Kerviel had "breached five levels of internal controls" in order to commit his offences and that he was a "computer genius".[157]

Kerviel himself offered a starkly different version of events. In an interview with the German magazine *Der Spiegel*, he claimed that SG was not only aware of the kind of trading activities he was involved in, but that it encouraged them. The magnitude of his buccaneering bets was drawn to their attention via an email in 2007, as well as his practice of concealing his positions by offsetting them with fictitious trades with nonexistent counterparties. Over the course of 2007, many more emails were sent to his superiors but rather than disciplining Kerviel, he alleges they merely told him that he should "take care of the problem."[158]

Instead of using his programmer's knowhow to circumvent SG's system, Kerviel went on to say that it was actually his bosses who had deactivated the risk controls on his computer, removing the $125 million exposure limit then in force on his trading desk. While it is not possible to establish the truth of these allegations, which the bank has consistently denied, it does seem strange that he was able to trade beyond their official limits for so many months before the final catastrophic ending brought his activities to light.

At one point, Kerviel was actually doing rather well with his unofficial trades. By January 2008, he had amassed a gain of €1.4 billion.[159] It is important to stress that he was not profiting personally from these trades and did not stand to do so, beyond an annual bonus of a few hundred thousand euros. His explanation was that he was doing it for the bank,[160] possibly in the hope of achieving superstar status within his department at SG and subsequent advancement and reward.

In October 2010, Kerviel was convicted of breach of trust, forgery and unauthorised use of computer systems, and was sentenced to three years imprisonment and symbolically ordered to repay the €4.9 billion that he had lost. He is now appealing his conviction. However, he was not tried for the more serious offence of attempted fraud, as prosecutors had originally desired.[161] In an internal audit in May 2008, SG branded Kerviel's immediate superiors as "deficient" and admitted that the bank had failed to follow up at least 74 internal trading alerts starting in mid-2006.[162]

Had it not been for the extreme moves in the stock market in early 2008, it is quite possible that Kerviel might have ended up with even fatter profits than he had already made, rather than those vast losses. One can easily imagine a scene in which a young trader is called in by his grinning bosses to receive a mock reprimand for some minor breach of internal procedure, which is then immediately forgotten about. And what better mitigating circumstances than a profit of several billion euros? It is surely not beyond the realms of possibility that there are several other Kerviels out there whose under-the-radar speculation earned them internal stardom and wealth, and who continue to operate today, albeit now with the full blessing and backing of their employer.

There are clearly some perverse incentives at work in this process. The rewards for success are potentially very large indeed, as Kerviel proved for a time. The employer is often the prime beneficiary in these cases, although financial institutions never disclose to the world the profits realised from winning rogue traders. When things go wrong, however, it is the taxpayer and innocent consumers that foot the bill. The other lesson from rogue trading in recent years is that instant personal gain is not always the motive. These individuals may be playing a longer game of first acquiring recognition for their skills, with the hope of riches and promotion later on.

INSIDER TRADERS

WHEREAS GIANT PONZI SCHEMERS may actually revel in the limelight and rogue traders aspire to receiving kudos on their own trading floor, insider traders never seek widespread recognition. The misuse of privileged information is illegal in most developed stock markets, often punishable by a combination of imprisonment, forfeiture of ill-gotten proceeds and permanent banishment from the financial services industry. Insider traders therefore operate in a shadowy underworld, making sure to discuss their precious illicit information either face-to-face or on their unrecorded personal mobile phones, and using friends and relatives to place the trades on their behalf.

The most obvious motivation of the users of insider information is money. Acting upon non-public knowledge that a company is about to be the subject of a takeover bid, or will shortly announce profits that are significantly below the market's expectations, can produce outsize profits. However, financial gain may not be the only force at work here, or at least perhaps not in quite the way that we would expect.

THE MOTIVATION OF INSIDER TRADERS

According to a study by Utpal Bhattacharya and Cassandra D. Marshall of Indiana University, insider trading is concentrated in the upper echelons of the corporate universe. In a rational world, where people commit crimes whose benefits outweigh the costs, logic dictates that it is lower management that would do the most insider trading. After all, such lower managers have less to lose in terms of reputation and future salary foregone in the event that they get caught. Exploring indictments for insider trading in the 1989 to 2002 period, however, Bhattacharya and Marshall found that it was the corporate top-brass that was most heavily involved. They concluded this was still true even allowing for the possibility that the authorities spend more time and resources on investigating the bigwigs.

The motivation of those who provide inside information to others may not be primarily financial, therefore. Admittedly, the provider may well expect a kickback from the grateful recipient of his tip, at least in certain instances. However, no money or other tangible reward changes hands in some cases. Imparting useful information to another person can enhance one's standing in the recipient's eyes. In turn, this can help to open doors for the tipster into elite social circles, for example. Bhattacharya and Marshall cite hubris, envy and arrogance as other emotions driving insider trading.

RAJ RAJARATNAM

Financial motivation certainly seems to have been uppermost in the case of Raj Rajaratnam and the Galleon Group hedge fund that he ran. During his trial for insider trading, it transpired that Rajaratnam had been in cahoots with Anil Kumar, who picked up privileged information in the course of his work as a technology advisor for McKinsey, the management consultancy. The two men had a longstanding association, having attended Wharton Business School together. Rajaratnam would pay his former classmate in return for tips.

The self-made billionaire, who at one time was the 236th richest person in the US, initially groomed his old friend with flattery. "You have such good knowledge that is worth a lot of money to me," Rajaratnam told Kumar, before persuading him to become his *consultant*. Each clearly realised that this was not a bona fide arrangement, however, at least going by the lengths they went to conceal Kumar's remuneration. Payments of $2m to Kumar were channelled via an offshore bank account in the name of his housekeeper.[163]

The strength of the personal connections between Rajaratnam, Kumar and the other defendants was a recurrent theme throughout the case. Rajiv Goel was a middling executive at Intel, the multinational maker of microchips. As Goel pleaded guilty to conspiracy and securities fraud, he outlined their relationship: "We studied together at Wharton. We kept in touch and our families went on vacations together." To Goel, supplying his friend Rajaratnam with corporate secrets was an extension of the other mutual assistance they provided: "We helped each other with our kids, their colleges – that [the tipping] was another way of helping each other out."[164]

Robert Moffat

Personal considerations were at the very heart of the case of Robert Moffat, an executive at IBM, the giant technology firm, who was convicted in 2010 as part of an investigation into Galleon Group. Moffat was having an extramarital affair with Danielle Chiesi, a former beauty queen turned hedge-fund manager. In the course of their trysts, Moffat gave Chiesi sensitive details of disappointing sales of IBM servers, a forthcoming restructuring at AMD and earnings at Lenovo. Moffat gained nothing financially from tipping off Chiesi. His lawyer gave a possible insight into his mindset:

> "Perhaps his ego got in the way by making him want to impress someone with whom he had become intimate. Perhaps he just wanted to seem knowledgeable and worldly."[165]

All these individuals received custodial sentences and suffered professional ruin. It may seem odd, then, that they were willing to commit the offences that they did, especially since they were already successful in their own right. This is especially so in the case of Robert Moffat, who stood to gain no material benefit from his illegal indiscretion. However, while the penalties are severe for insider trading, the risk of detection is small. Between late 2009 and February 2012, there were a mere 57 successful prosecutions for this behaviour in the United States. It seems most unlikely that this represents anything other than the tip of iceberg.

CLUES FROM PRICE AND VOLUME DATA

Price and volume data from the stock market can offer us some vital clues as to the extent of insider trading activity. Corporate takeover bids are a favourite event for insider traders, since the stock price of the target company typically spikes dramatically once the offer is made public. Insiders of the target companies involved naturally come under close scrutiny therefore. Nevertheless, they do alter their trading behaviour in advance of their firms receiving offers. According to a study of some 3,700 takeovers between 1988 and 2006, US company insiders were observed to have increased their net purchases of their own stock by reducing the amount of stock they sold in the year leading up to the takeover.[166]

Of necessity, the most egregious – and most lucrative – cases of insider trading take place at one remove or further from the company officers themselves. It is the corporate insiders' friends, family, lovers and fellow business-school alumni who are best placed to take advantage of juicy titbits, while running much less risk of detection. Numerous studies have demonstrated that trading volumes spike to abnormal levels in the days preceding a takeover bid.[167] These trades are obviously not the direct work of company officers, but of those to whom they have entrusted their classified knowledge.

Prevalence of crime

It often feels as if financial crime is more prevalent today than ever before. At the top end, these crimes certainly seem to have become ever larger and more frequent. The increasing complexity and sophistication of the financial world may be one of the reasons for this. The proliferation of financial derivative products – with their ability to turn small price moves into much larger returns – is one element of this trend. And while the internet age has given ordinary investors access to levels of information that previous generations never had, it has also provided a new means for fraudsters to target millions of individuals in ways that Oscar Hartzell would have dearly loved.

Apart from the vastly expanded possibilities for committing financial crime, the temptation to do so has become greater too. The gap between the richest and others in society in the US and some other places has returned to levels last seen in the 1920s. At the same time, wealth is more conspicuous than ever before. Ferraris and other dream-machines are now a daily sight on the streets of London, New York and other financial centres. To join the ranks of this privileged elite demands special skill, extraordinary luck, or particular deviousness. Ambitious folk lacking either of the first two of these qualities frequently fall back upon the latter.

Endnotes

134 *Financial Times* (30 June 2008).

135 *New York Times* (7 March 2012).

136 'Two Knights of Honour', Caribbean 360 (November 2006).

137 *Daily Telegraph* (2 November 2009).

138 *Washington Post* (12 Dec 2008).

139 Mitchell Zuckoff, CNN Money (5 January 2009).

140 Samuel Freedman, 'Trust and Exploitation in a Close-Knit World', *New York Times* (7 December 2008).

[141] 'Madoff had a steady presence on Capitol Hill', *Los Angeles Times* (22 December 2008).

[142] Michael Freedman, *New York Times* (7 December 2008).

[143] *Wall Street Journal* (5 January 2009).

[144] Freedman, *New York Times* (7 December 2008).

[145] Prof. Steven Pressman, 'On Financial Frauds and their Causes', *American Journal of Economics and Sociology* (October 1998).

[146] See for example, George Akerlof, Michael Spence and Joseph Stiglitz 'The Market for "Lemons": Quality Uncertainty and the Market Mechanism', *Quarterly Journal of Economics* 84:3 (August 1970).

[147] Pressman, 'On Financial Frauds'.

[148] Pressman, 'On Financial Frauds'.

[149] *Christianity Today* (19 June 1995).

[150] *Financial Times* (12 December 2008), based on Podcast interview with Matthew Vincent.

[151] *Wall Street Journal* (5 January 2009).

[152] *Washington Post* (12 December 2008).

[153] CBS News (1 March 2009).

[154] *USA Today* (15 December 2008).

[155] *Wall Street Journal* (22 December 2008).

[156] Nick Leeson, *Rogue Trader: How I Brought Down Barings Bank and Shook the Financial World* (Sphere, new edition, 1999).

[157] Nicola Clark and David Jolly, 'Fraud Costs Bank $7.1 Billion', *New York Times* (25 January 2008).

[158] *Der Spiegel* (16 November 2010).

[159] 'Rogue trader began year in profit', BBC (30 January 2008).

[160] 'Accused rogue trader Kerviel says he didn't invent his betting tricks', Associated Press (9 June 2010).

[161] Nicola Clark, 'Rogue Trader at Société Générale Gets 3 Years', New York Times (5 October 2010).

[162] 'Jérôme Kerviel', *New York Times* (5 October 2010).

[163] *Wall Street Journal* (14 March 2012).

[164] Courtney Comstock, 'Rajiv Goel At The Raj Trial: "I Had To Use The Money Raj Gave Me To Clear Out An Infestation Of Rats" ', *Business Insider* (22 March 2011).

[165] *Wall Street Journal* (14 March 2012).

[166] Anup Agrawal, University of Alabama, and Tareque Nasser, Kansas State University, 'Insider Trading in Takeover Targets' (2012).

[167] Gregg Jarrell, *Washington Post* (17 December 1986).

CHAPTER 10

CENTRAL BANKS: LEAVE, IMPROVE OR ABOLISH?

BANKERS OF EVERY VARIETY have suffered a spectacular fall from grace in the early 21st century. Since the credit crisis erupted in 2007, they have attracted fierce and unrelenting criticism around the world. Commercial bankers have been panned for their reckless lending to unfit homebuyers and investment bankers have been derisively dismissed as *casino speculators* who destabilise the economy. Perhaps the most scathing words of all have been directed at those at the very heart of the financial system: the central bankers.

Central banks stand accused of having perverted or failed in all of their main purposes, these being managing the money supply, overseeing the banking industry and acting as lenders of last resort. These alleged sins are said to have contributed to – and perhaps even to have caused – the disastrous credit bubbles and busts in Japan in the 1980s and then in the West from 2007.

The debate over the role of central bankers in the credit crisis has since developed into scrutiny of their activities during normal times. In particular, much has been made of their part both in creating inflation over the long run and in exacerbating the repetitive cycle of boom and bust in the economy. All this raises the ultimate question of whether central banks should continue to exist at all, or at least whether they should remain in their current form.

Central bankers are, of course, famous for their delicate – and sometimes even Delphic – utterances. After all, a poorly-chosen phrase or even a slight overemphasis within a public statement can have profound effects on the financial markets that hang on their every announcement. Despite this habit of cautious speech, however, central bankers are charged with having been decidedly incautious in their attitude to three of the most critical events of recent decades.

CENTRAL BANKS AT CENTRE STAGE

THE JAPANESE BOOM of the 1980s, the technology mania of the late 1990s and the housing bubble of the early 2000s all culminated in wealth destruction on a massive scale. Aside from these wealth effects, Japan has suffered more than two decades of economic dislocation since 1989 and the US housing bust that began in 2006 – and real-estate crashes in other nations – threaten to create a *lost era*, similar to Japan's, in the West.

JAPANESE BOOM OF THE 1980S AND TECHNOLOGY BOOM OF THE 1990S

All three of the speculative manias just mentioned were several years in the making and in each instance there were clear signs that things were getting out of hand well before the final collapse. For example, Japan's Nikkei 225 index exploded upwards by 114 per cent in the three years to its record peak in December 1989. The Japanese stock market traded on more than 50 times trailing earnings during this period, compared to an average of around 21 times between 1973 and 1985.[168]

The power of central bankers to influence the course of bubbles like this is in little doubt. In December 1996, Federal Reserve Chairman Alan Greenspan gave an after-dinner speech in which he posed the rhetorical question: "But how do we know when irrational exuberance has unduly escalated asset values, which then become subject to unexpected and prolonged contractions as they have in Japan over the past decade?"[169] In the immediate aftermath of this address, financial markets tumbled on the insinuation from the world's most powerful central banker.

However, Mr Greenspan did not follow up these words with any action, or even with further words on the matter. Exuberance among investors developed into outright euphoria. America's S&P 500 index more than doubled from the time of his 1996 speech to its then-record peak in March 2000. And the NASDAQ Composite index – home of many high-technology companies – quadrupled during the same period.

While Alan Greenspan and the Federal Reserve remained silent on the speculative excesses in technology, media and telecoms, many outside of the US central bank were more vocal. In early 2000, Robert Shiller, a Yale economist, published a best-selling book warning that American equities were significantly overvalued. Poignantly, he took Mr Greenspan's "irrational exuberance" quotation as the title of his work.

Professor Shiller – as well as many other academic and professional observers – were subsequently vindicated in their view of the stock mania. Between March 2000 and October 2002, the S&P 500 shed half of its total value and the NASDAQ Composite lost almost four-fifths. Even after this carnage, Mr Greenspan and other Fed officials denied that they could have done more. "It was very difficult to definitively identify a bubble until after the fact – that is, when its bursting confirmed its existence," said Mr Greenspan in August 2002.[170]

The fallout from the technology bubble's collapse was much less severe than from that of the ending of Japan's mania a decade earlier. America suffered a recession in 2001 that was so mild that it had ended before economists could even agree that it had begun. But the consequences of the next asset-price frenzy would be much more far-reaching – both for the economy and for the central bankers.

A BUBBLE INFLATES IN THE HOUSING MARKET

Although the technology bubble had only just deflated, a housing market bubble was expanding its place, both in the US and in numerous other countries around the world. Home prices in 20 metropolitan areas more than doubled between early 2000 and mid-2006.[171] Certain local markets – such as Las Vegas – recorded even headier increases.

Once again, however, the Federal Reserve downplayed suggestions that the housing market was becoming detached from reality. In 2005, Ben Bernanke, then a Federal Reserve Governor who was shortly to succeed Alan Greenspan as Chairman, was quizzed about rampant home-price gains by a journalist. When asked if he thought there was a bubble in residential real estate, Mr Bernanke responded in the negative, claiming that he thought the price rises were essentially justified.

> "I think it's important to note that fundamentals are also very strong," he said. "We've got a growing economy, jobs, incomes. We've got very low mortgage rates. We've got demographics supporting housing growth. We've got restricted supply in some places. So it's certainly understandable that prices would go up some. I don't know whether prices are exactly where they should be, but I think it's fair to say that much of what's happened is supported by the strength of the economy."[172]

Tempting fate, Mr Bernanke went on to point out that America had never before suffered a nationwide decline in home values and predicted that growth would merely slow or stabilise. Within a year of these remarks, the catastrophic bust in US housing was underway. Rather than stabilising, the S&P Case-Shiller index of 20 cities shed one-third between July 2006 and October 2011. The losses were sufficiently widespread to qualify as America's first nationwide crash.

How central banks respond to events

Even if Mr Greenspan was correct in his contention that bubbles are not easy for central banks to identify, this still leaves the matter of how central banks should respond once they do actually burst. Failing to warn the markets of mounting risks of excessive speculation might be considered unfortunate, failing to deal adequately with its aftermath is surely much harder to excuse.

The inaction of the Bank of Japan

Since the Japanese boom turned to bust in late 1989, the country has suffered more than two decades of economic strife. Its economy has grown an average rate of just 0.85 per cent a year, compared to 4.5 per cent a year in the decade preceding the crisis.[173] As well as weak growth, recessions were frequent, with eight contractions between 1990 and 2011. (The US suffered just three, by contrast.) At the start of 2012, the Nikkei 225 stock index remained more than three-quarters below its 1989 peak. Consumer price growth has stagnated at an average of 0.34 per cent annually.[174]

The Bank of Japan is widely blamed for its failure to address these persistent problems, particularly deflation. Although the Bank of Japan (BoJ) reduced interest rates from a high of six per cent in 1991 to 0.5 per cent in September 1995 – a level they have seldom exceeded since – there is a case that it should have gone much further. While Japan pioneered quantitative easing, it stands accused of failing to pursue this policy radically enough.

Just as both Greenspan and Bernanke were keen to play down the Federal Reserve's ability to address bubbles in the making, the BoJ has consistently tried to argue that the problem of deflation lies beyond its control. Masaaki Shirakawa, governor of the BoJ, has claimed that falling prices result primarily from the country's shrinking workforce and sliding productivity. Monetary measures like zero interest rates and quantitative easing are therefore only one part of the solution, in his view. His suggested remedies include swelling the labour-force and stimulating consumer demand with innovative new products.

Prior to 1998, the BoJ was under the effective control of the Ministry of Finance. Monetary policy during the bubble of the 1980s and the first few years of its aftermath was therefore as much a tool of politics as of economics. Indeed, critics have argued that both the bubble and the ineffective response to its bursting directly resulted from of a lack of central bank independence. The same cannot be said of either America's Federal Reserve or the ECB, both of whose decision-making is supposed to be free of outside political control.

TOO MUCH ACTION BY CENTRAL BANKS – CRITICISMS OF QE

Having struck 17 years earlier than the Western world's credit crunch of 2007, Japan's crisis had already been widely studied by central bankers elsewhere. Indeed, Ben Bernanke has long been of the view that Japan's deflationary crisis and America's Great Depression of the 1930s were needlessly worsened by the lack of robust action from the respective nations' central banks. Had only they loosened monetary policy aggressively, deflation might have been defeated and recovery achieved much earlier, he has argued.

In one respect, Mr Bernanke has succeeded in his prescribed policy. Few have accused the Federal Reserve of under-using the tools at its disposal in response to the most recent crisis. The Fed slashed short-term interest rates from 5.25 per cent at the outset of the crunch in August 2007 to a low of 0.25 per cent by December 2008, a level at which they remained into early 2012. It also engaged in aggressive money-printing from early 2009 into mid-2011. By contrast, the BoJ waited six years after deflation first appeared before resorting to the printing presses.

Rather than attacking the Federal Reserve and the Bank of England (BoE) for doing too little, the main charge levelled against these banks is that they have done *too much*. The Fed's first and second rounds of QE amounted to $2.3 trillion, while the BoE's efforts to early 2012 totalled £275bn. In proportion to the size of the US and UK economies, these programmes were far bigger than anything that Japan has carried out.

To believers in sound money, central banks' policy of creating trillions out of thin air can only end in one way; runaway inflation. Uncontrolled price increases are even more pernicious than price declines, it is argued, as they disproportionately injure the vulnerable, such as retirees who live off their savings and low-paid workers who have little wage-bargaining power.

Such attacks on quantitative easing rang particularly true in the UK. Whereas inflation in the US stayed fairly restrained following QE – at least according to official statistics – the same cannot be said for Britain. The retail price index rose at more than five per cent in 2011, despite the economy growing feebly and unemployment rising sharply.

The difficulty for central bankers lies in proving the counterfactual case: how would things have turned out had it not been for quantitative easing? Defenders of QE on both sides of the Atlantic have claimed that without it, the US and UK may indeed have lapsed into outright deflation. James Ferguson of Arbuthnot, a London investment house, estimated in late 2011 that the UK money supply would have shrunk by 13 per cent and consumer prices would have declined in absence of the BoE's efforts.[175]

Aside from the creation of inflation, a commonly-laid charge against QE is that it has largely benefited a select and already-unpopular few, namely investment bankers and hedge-fund managers. Within this argument, the freshly-created cash from the central banks largely ends up in the hands of professional speculators, who recycle it into highly profitable bets on equities, commodities and other risky assets, such as high-end property and artwork. Meanwhile, jobs continue to be lost in the wider economy and real incomes are eroded by inflation. Put simply, QE can appear to be aimed less at benefiting the guy on Main Street and more at further enriching the mensch in the Hamptons.

Criticism of the ECB

Refraining from quantitative easing is no recipe for a central bank to achieve popularity, however. Throughout the 2009-2011 period, the ECB consciously shied away from the money-printing and bond-buying activities of the Fed, BoJ, BoE and others. Not only is the ECB forbidden from buying debt directly from European governments, it is also under enormous pressure from its largest member state, Germany, not to engage in anything that even looks like QE. In the face of deteriorating economic fundamentals and financial-market seize-up, the ECB's resolve has drawn criticism from many sides.

Paul de Grauwe, a professor of economics at the University of Leuven, memorably equated the ECB's policy to an *act of self-imposed chastity*. Writing shortly after an extreme bout of market nerves in October 2011, he pointed out that the European sovereign debt crisis had degenerated into a banking crisis. "The ECB has no excuse not to act [by printing money]," he wrote. "In trying to keep its monetary virginity intact, the bank threatens to destroy the eurozone. If that happens, nobody will be able to profit from its virginity."[176]

Tellingly, his remarks were subsequently echoed by an outgoing ECB official in December 2011. Lorenzo Bini Smaghi said he did not understand the "quasi-religious discussions about quantitative easing." He went on to say that QE would be appropriate in particular "for countries facing a liquidity-trap that may lead to deflation." At the time, Mr Smaghi's home country of Italy looked especially at risk of being unable to service its substantial debts and of suffering a prolonged recession as a result of austerity measures.[177]

CENTRAL BANK MONETARY POLICY AND THE CREATION OF BUBBLES

HOWEVER, CENTRAL BANKS may be guilty of a much more serious offence than merely failing to warn of bubbles or reacting ineffectively to their bursting. There is a growing body of opinion that says that central banks actually *caused* these wild speculative episodes through deliberate acts of policy – and then invited repeat disasters through their response to their fallout.

The mainstream explanation for the credit sprees in Japan in the 1980s, and in the West in the 1990s and 2000s, stresses the actions of commercial lenders and investment bankers. Commercial banks lent promiscuously – to inefficient businesses in Japan, and to unfit borrowers in the US. Investment bankers, meanwhile, created ostensibly clever – but fatally-flawed – derivatives that hid the true risks of much of this lending. The public got carried away with *animal spirits* and borrowed more than it should have done.

Economists of the Austrian school retort that this analysis underplays or even ignores the root cause of the problem. They argue that financial innovation and the madness of crowds are not sufficient in themselves to create a bubble. The lifeblood of any speculative mania, they say, is cheap credit. Commercial banks may make irresponsible loans, but they only do so because the central bank has enabled them to do thus.

The Austrians claim that central banks persistently set interest rates at much lower levels than they would have been set by the free market. These artificially low interest rates persuade people and firms to undertake marginal business projects and purchase financial assets that they otherwise would not have considered worthwhile. The more credit there is created in this way, the greater the mal-investment that occurs.

Within this explanation, what goes up must come down. The central bank's credit-fuelled boom inevitably leads to a painful bust. As the mal-investment becomes increasingly apparent and credit then dries up, the speculation goes into reverse. The weaker businesses and lowest-quality securities fall hard in value. According to the Austrians, the resulting liquidation of assets and recession is the natural result of the market restoring balance after the excesses of the credit boom.

Although the Austrian school is on the fringe of economic thought, its ideas have attracted increasing attention since the eruption of the credit crisis in 2007. Even so, its theories about central-bank behaviour – and about much else – are still roundly rejected by many mainstream economists. In particular, the Austrian premise that businesses and consumers would repeatedly make the same erroneous choices in response to artificially low interest rates is dismissed as nonsensical.

While those outside of the Austrian school do not make the same strident denunciations of central banks' role in bubbles and busts, they do admit that cheap credit has a part to play. Empirical studies of manias throughout the ages typically have addressed this phenomenon. In relation to Britain's stock-market boom of the 1690s – which followed shortly after the establishment of the Bank of England as the first central bank – Edward Chancellor, a financial historian wrote:

> "Credit was in constant flux, elusive, independent, and uncontrollable... Credit was the Siamese twin of speculation; they were born at the same time and exhibited the same nature; inextricably linked they could never be totally separated."[178]

THE BOJ STOKES THE JAPANESE CRISIS

The Bank of Japan's policies are widely acknowledged as a major factor within Japan's mega-boom in the 1980s. The real cost of borrowing fell sharply in Japan in the late 1980s, even as the economy was growing strongly. Adjusted for inflation, the BoJ's interest rate came down from 4.2 per cent at the start of 1987 to a low of just 0.3 per cent in June 1989, just six months before the bubble burst.[179]

As we have already seen, the contemporary signs that the situation was getting out of control were obvious. Aside from the doubling of the stock market within three years, real-estate prices grew explosively. Residential land in six of Japan's big cities more than doubled from the end of 1986 to late 1990.[180] At the height of the frenzy, it was famously estimated that the 7.4 km² grounds of the Imperial Palace in Tokyo were worth more than the entire value of the US state of California, which covers 423,970 km². Memberships to certain golf clubs were sold for $4m apiece and were worth as much as $200bn in aggregate.

The BoJ's decision to lower interest rates in 1987 amidst an almighty boom was equivalent to pouring petrol on a fire. But the country's central bank may have had little choice, given that it was effectively controlled by the Ministry of Finance. The United States applied pressure on the Japanese government to stimulate domestic consumption in order to reduce its large current-account surplus with America. The Ministry of Finance is therefore widely blamed for forcing the central bank into a policy-error.

While the BoJ was not to gain its formal independence for another decade, there is an argument that it was acting more of its own volition than is widely understood. Ryunoshin Kamikawa of Osaka University has suggested[181] that rather than caving into pressure from government at the behest of the United States, the BoJ had a more legitimate agenda. He suggests that the BoJ feared a recession could occur in Japan, triggered by the country's sharply strengthening currency.

THE FED AND ECB

Lack of independence from government is a less credible defence for the central banks of the US, the UK and the eurozone, however. As in Japan, these three institutions pursued very loose monetary policy in the early 21st century. At that time, all enjoyed day-to-day freedom in setting rates. The Fed and ECB had been officially independent since their creation in 1913 and 1998 respectively, while the BoE gained its own powers in 1997.

Haunted by the recent experience of Japan in the 1990s, the Fed under Alan Greenspan cut interest rates aggressively when the technology bubble imploded in 2000. From their millennium-year peak of 6.5 per cent, rates came down to a then-record low of one per cent by mid-2003. This helped sustain consumer spending during the period, leading to a comparatively mild recession and a rampant recovery from late 2002. Although the Fed began raising rates from mid-2004, the hikes were small and gradual.

Federal Reserve interest-rate policy between early 2001 and early 2006 was much looser than one leading economic rule-of-thumb suggested that it should have been, according to the World Bank.[182] The Taylor Rule says that the interest rate ought to reflect whether inflation and unemployment are above or below target, and the level of interest rates that is consistent with full employment. This period of monetary laxity was, of course, the period when US home prices took off sharply.

Both Alan Greenspan and Ben Bernanke deny that Fed policy during this period was excessively loose. Instead, they attribute low interest rates largely to outside forces over which they had no influence. In a 2005 speech, Mr Bernanke claimed that a "global savings glut" was responsible for low interest rates, rather than Federal Reserve Policy.[183] In his view, interest rates were low because there were too many savings – especially in Asia – chasing too few investment opportunities.

This argument was given short shrift by many economists, both Austrian-school and others. In particular, John B. Taylor – a Stanford economics professor and creator of the eponymous interest-rate rule – pointed out that total world savings were actually around multi-year lows compared to the size of the world economy during the 2002 to 2004 period of very low interest rates.[184]

Compared to the Federal Reserve, the ECB probably had less room for manoeuvre in the early 2000s. Economic performance among the eurozone's then 12 member countries was a very mixed bag. Faced with sluggish growth in Germany and Italy – the bloc's first and third largest economies – the ECB kept rates very low in order to stimulate recovery. From a peak of 4.75 per cent in May 2001, the ECB slashed its main refinancing rate to two per cent by June 2003. It then kept rates at that level until the end of 2005.

These low rates did eventually help bring about a powerful recovery in Germany. However, they also stoked wild speculative booms in the already-expanding economies of Spain and Ireland. House prices in Spain soared by 145 per cent from the start of 2001 to their peak in mid-2007, while those in Ireland went up 80 per cent over the same period.[185] New construction reached breakneck pace, with more new housing units under construction in Spain in 2006 than in Germany, France, Italy and the UK combined.[186]

These episodes ended extremely painfully as interest rates were raised to more normal levels and the credit crunch then struck in 2007. Spanish home prices had shed almost a quarter by the end of 2011, although statisticians believe this understates the true decline in the market. In some areas, values had fallen by half from their peak levels. For Ireland as a whole, government figures in early 2011 noted a drop of 35 per cent from the 2007 peak, with Dublin property down 47 per cent.

While accepting that primary responsibility lay at home, John Bruton, who led Ireland's government between 1994 and 1997, said that the European Central Bank had displayed a "major failure of prudential supervision" in relation to Ireland's bubble. Despite clear signs of spiralling house prices, and the eagerness of commercial banks from elsewhere in Europe to lend to Irish developers, the ECB "seemingly raised no objection to this lending."[187]

CENTRAL BANK MONETARY POLICY IN NORMAL CONDITIONS

CRITICISM OF THE CENTRAL BANKS' part in the bubble of the early 2000s has also raised fundamental questions about their role under more normal conditions. While vast amounts of wealth were eradicated in the relatively short periods of the Japanese slump and the collapse of the international technology and real-estate bubbles, this is small fry compared to the value-destruction resulting from inflation over the long run.

INFLATION

Since the establishment of the Bank of England in 1694, the British pound has lost 99.9 per cent of its purchasing power.[188] The US dollar is worth 96 per cent less in real terms than when the Federal Reserve opened its doors in 1913.[189] The euro, meanwhile, buys almost 30 per cent less than it did at the time of its launch in 1999.[190] The causes of inflation are one of the most contentious issues in economics, but most theorists allow at least some role for the central banks in the inflationary process.

The basic proposition is simple enough. When too much money chases too few goods, the result is inflation. Professor Milton Friedman, the leading economist of the monetarist school, argued that "inflation is always and everywhere a monetary phenomenon".

In other words, the responsibility for the creation of too much money – and the resulting inflation – lies with its issuers: the central banks.

Sceptics argue that the truth is more nuanced than it being "always and everywhere" a problem created by those who control the money supply. They point out, for example, that both costs and demand can increase without more money being created. But the central banks can hardly be blameless. To take an extreme example, the Zimbabwean authorities are universally held responsible – except only by themselves – for the hyperinflation that reached 11.2 million per cent in 2008. At the behest of Zimbabwe's government, the Reserve Bank of Zimbabwe literally printed vast amounts of new banknotes for the express purpose of meeting the government's expenses.

CYCLES OF BOOM AND BUST

Inflation, however, is just one aspect of the distortion to the economy that central banks are accused of creating. Central banks' most fierce critics – the Austrian school – say they are also responsible for a large part of the repetitive cycle of boom and bust that occurs over time. They are said to do this in the same way that they create the spectacular bubbles and crashes.

The process begins when central banks lower interest rates excessively, creating a false impression that there are lots of savings available for investment. Businesses are hoodwinked into borrowing to undertake investment projects that would have been unprofitable at a more realistic rate of interest. Ultimately, the credit expansion ends as the pool of business and speculation opportunities dries up. The weaker businesses go bust and the most speculative investments plunge in value as recession takes hold.

While mainstream economists reject the notion that central banks' activities are the main factor driving the business cycle, they do admit that policy errors can have a big impact on growth. Aside from running excessively loose monetary policy at inappropriate times, central banks have also frequently committed the opposite error of prematurely or excessively raising rates.

Even while Japanese consumer prices were falling, the recently independent Bank of Japan decided to raise interest rates in 2000. The Japanese economy suffered a year-long recession starting in 2001 and deflation worsened. At the first signs of an end to deflation in 2006, it raised rates twice, which was followed by a lapse back into deflation in 2007. On each occasion, there were ample calls from politicians and economists not to act as the BoJ did. But while the BoJ exercised its independence, it did so at the expense of its deflation-busting mandate.

The ECB's decision to raise interest rates in July 2011 was also met with incredulity in many quarters. At the time, there was a clear threat of recession in much of the eurozone, while investors were terrified that Greece might default on its government debt. Nonetheless, the ECB hiked its benchmark rate from 1.25 to 1.5 per cent. At the time, David Blanchflower, a former interest-rate setter at the Bank of England, described the move as a "classic policy error [which] will exacerbate the growth problems experienced by all countries."[191] By reversing the hike a mere four months later, the ECB implicitly acknowledged its misjudgement.

HOW THE SINS OF CENTRAL BANKS MIGHT BE CORRECTED

Identifying the alleged sins of central banks is much easier than determining how to correct them. The possibilities range from leaving them very much as they are to scrapping them altogether. In the middle of the spectrum is changing central banks' mandates or their powers. But there is little agreement about how best to achieve any of these options – particularly the most radical solution of abolition.

MAINTAINING THE STATUS QUO

There is at least some chance that central banking will continue more or less in its current form. This depends largely on the fate of the financial system and world economies over the coming years. Consider a positive scenario under which quantitative easing by the central banks helps to avoid a repetition (or worse) of the panic of 2008, a prolonged Japanese-style decade or more of lost growth is avoided in the developed world and recovery occurs without QE provoking either persistently high inflation or even hyperinflation.

Were events to follow this course, it is likely that society in a decade's time would judge the central bankers rather more kindly than it does now. Some observers have even anticipated such an outcome already. In an interview in 2009, Jim Cramer, the maverick Wall Street commentator and investor, argued that Ben Bernanke had "saved the Western world." In his view, we were "at a precipice, as we will discover in later years, when we were a few days from your ATM machine not working."[192]

There are precedents of central banks enduring major periods of unpopularity but ultimately emerging with their reputations enhanced. Faced with the nightmarish combination of high inflation and weak economic growth, the Federal Reserve raised interest rates to a peak of 20 per cent in 1981. This measure contributed to a savage US recession, which brought great hardship to businesses and workers in the most economically-sensitive areas of the economy.

The Fed – personified by its then-Chairman Paul Volcker – became one of the most vilified institutions in America. Mr Volcker received piles of lumber daubed with angry messages from workless carpenters and mailbags stuffed full of the keys of unsalable vehicles from carmakers. Farmers famously rode into Washington on tractors and blockaded the Fed's headquarters, while homebuilders in Kentucky put up wanted posters featuring mugshots of Volcker and his fellow-governors.[193]

However, the so-called *Volcker shock* successfully brought inflation under control. Price-growth declined from its peak of 13.5 per cent a year in 1981 to around three per cent in 1983. Inflation in the US has remained largely under control ever since. Even today, Mr Volcker enjoys the best – or least tarnished – record of any Federal Reserve Chairman of the last half-century.

GOVERNMENTS COULD PARE BACK CENTRAL BANK INDEPENDENCE

Governments could always reclaim some or all of the powers that they originally granted central banks. According to Daniel Hannan – a prominent British free-marketeer and Member of the European Parliament – "the [Bank of England's] Monetary Policy Committee has failed spectacularly, and should be abolished." Rather than being an independent organ, as it is billed, Mr Hannan says the BoE's MPC is a quango.

The Bank of England's crime in Mr Hannan's eyes is to have kept UK interest rates artificially low and to have printed money during the 2009 to 2011 period. Had the Treasury been setting interest rates, as it did before 1997, he would have liked it to have raised rates. But while Mr Hannan believes in monetary rigour, there is no guarantee that other politicians would take such a high-minded approach.

When a government directly controls monetary policy, it has an inevitable temptation to set interest rates according to its electoral needs. As polling day looms on the horizon, it may attempt to boost employment with rate-cuts, thereby improving its prospects at the ballot-box. Despite the credit crisis, the consensus in the UK remains that an independent central bank is more trustworthy than the government would be.

GREATER TRANSPARENCY AND ACCOUNTABILITY

Ending central bank independence is unlikely and probably also undesirable. But there is an appetite for trying to make central banks more transparent and accountable to the public. "Congress and the American people have minimal, if any, oversight over trillions of dollars that the Fed controls," says Ron Paul, a libertarian US politician and sometime Presidential candidate.[194] Both in their day-to-day activities – and during emergencies – the Fed and other central banks operate under a shroud of secrecy.

A routine example of central-bank secrecy is the practice of delaying the release of the minutes of their meetings, typically for some days. Central banks defend this practice on the grounds that it gives them the ability to make surprising policy changes for the good of society. This might include a monetary expansion at a time when popular opinion wants, but doesn't expect, such a move.[195]

Operational secrecy can be much further-reaching and less benign than this, though. In 2008, the Federal Reserve made as much as $1.2 trillion worth of loans at low or zero interest rates to various American and overseas commercial banks. However, the Fed refused to disclose the identity of the borrowers until August 2011, and only then after court action and changes in legislation.[196]

In court in May 2009, the Fed argued that its wall of silence was necessary to prevent a bank run. If it were disclosed that banks were turning to the system's lender of last resort, it could "fuel market speculation and rumours that the entity's liquidity strains stem from a financial problem at the institution that is not publicly known." But while preventing bank runs is clearly desirable, this behaviour can equally be interpreted as central banks protecting the banks' interests rather than those of the public.

The impression of an overly cosy relationship between the Fed and the banking industry is reinforced by the September 2008 bailout of American International Group (AIG), the stricken insurance group. When AIG executives met with the Treasury and

Fed officials at the Federal Reserve Bank of New York, also in attendance was Lloyd Blankfein, chief executive of Goldman Sachs. AIG subsequently received more than $182bn in taxpayer funds, of which $13 billion went to ensure that Goldman Sachs avoided losses.

"The most powerful entity in the United States [the Fed] is riddled with conflicts of interest," said Bernie Sanders, a US Senator, in late 2011.[197] The Government Accountability Office – America's public audit office – seemed to agree that reputational risks might be posed. It identified at least 18 current and former Fed board-members with ties to banks and firms that received Fed help during the credit crunch. It recommended the Fed recruit from a broader pool of candidates and make public its bylaws and other governance documents.

Simply making central banks more accountable may not be enough, though. There is a case that central banking is fundamentally flawed as an activity. As long as it exists, therefore, society is condemned to suffer cycles of boom and bust, persistent inflation, and cronyism between central and other bankers. If this really is the case, the only solution is to abolish central banking altogether.

Abolishing central banks outright

Abolishing central banking ultimately means doing away with the entire monetary system that goes with it. Instead of having a state-monopoly supplier of money that can create currency from thin air, money could be privatised. Commercial banks – and maybe even others – would therefore issue their own money. This money would necessarily be very different from the sort of money that circulates today.

To prevent private issuers of money from creating unlimited credit on a whim, their money would have to be backed up, i.e.

convertible into something else. The Austrian school of economics believes that gold – and perhaps also silver – would serve best. Whereas today's commercial banks can make loans worth many times the value of the deposits they take from savers, this would not be possible under a totally-backed currency, as it would be obliged to redeem its banknotes into gold or silver on demand.

A RETURN TO CURRENCY BACKED BY PRECIOUS METALS

To modern ears, the idea of a currency being convertible into precious metals can sound archaic. Opponents of the idea frequently invoke the Great Depression of the 1930s, which, they say, was exacerbated by countries keeping interest rates cripplingly high in a bid to defend their gold-backed currencies. Had they only resorted to paper money earlier, the Great Depression might have been much less severe. Countries like Britain that abandoned gold earlier emerged from the slump much sooner than countries like France that clung to it.

Practicality is another argument often heard against a currency convertible into precious metals. To settle transactions, say critics, banks would have to cart around large amounts of heavy metal, while consumers would be reluctant to do actual transactions using gold and silver. However, a central clearing-house system would help alleviate the first issue, while debit cards linked to gold would address the second.

Is a gold-backed currency really the antidote to inflation and the boom-and-bust cycle, as Austrian economists suggest? During the heyday of convertible money in the 19th century, consumer-price growth was indeed often very restrained or even negative. Following the end of the American civil war in 1865, consumer prices are estimated to have fallen in 22 of the following 35 years. During the gold-standard era in Britain from 1816 to 1914[198], the median rate of inflation was 0.2 per cent a year, with prices falling in just under half of all years.

Although deflation has come to be associated with slumps, this is not necessarily the case. While prices fell persistently for long periods in the 19th century, the US economy was actually growing rapidly. The US economy was around four times bigger in real terms in 1900 than it had been in 1865. Admittedly, America was essentially an emerging market at this point, and therefore growing much more quickly. The point is, though, that deflation and growth are far from incompatible.

Currency convertible into gold has a decent enough record of avoiding inflation, but what about the Austrian school's other contention, that it would also eliminate the repeating rhythm of boom and bust? There was very clearly a business cycle in gold-standard economies in the 19th and 20th centuries. And not only was there a business cycle, but quite a pronounced one. Despite the strong growth overall, the US suffered nine recessions from 1865 to 1900.[199] This included speculative manias and panics.

Although there was no Federal Reserve, convertible-money enthusiasts still blame boom-and-bust in those days upon abuses by the government and commercial banks. Paper money was only partly backed up by gold, they say, leaving scope for the same sort of credit creation from thin air that happens today. The remedy for this is for all money issued to have full gold backing.

Appetite for gold among the public has clearly grown massively since the end of the 20th century. The yellow metal's price rose 660 per cent from a multi-year low of $253 in July 1999 to $1,924 in September 2011. To satisfy demand from small buyers, a company in Germany in 2009 began offering coins, miniature bars and wafers from vending machines in public places.[200] But while consumers may have warmed to gold as a store of value, this doesn't necessarily prove they want a gold-backed currency.

THE PUBLIC APPETITE FOR A RETURN TO GOLD-BACKED CURRENCY

Insofar as there is a desire to abolish central banks and revert to money linked to gold, it is strongest in the US. In May 2011, the state of Utah passed a law making certain gold and silver coins legal tender. Other states have considered making similar laws. Utah's move was largely a symbolic gesture. Should inflation take off as a result of the Fed's money-creation efforts, however, it could eventually attain practical significance too.

ALTERNATIVE APPROACHES

Of course, there is no reason why a free currency must be backed by gold and silver specifically. Another possibility is that money could be linked to a broad bundle of goods, whose cost is similar to the general price level. Leland Yeager and Robert Greenfield, two US economists, have proposed just such a system, where the government plays little role and commodity prices are not driven by changes in the amount of money. Anyone wanting to redeem their money would not receive a basket of commodities, though, but perhaps gold or securities.

The advance of technology also provides further interesting possibilities of privately-issued money. Electronic payments have been around for many years and more recently the internet has enabled the birth of new digital currencies. The most famous of these are Bitcoins, a currency that has allowed users to pay one another for goods and services online since early 2009 with few or no transaction costs.

Bitcoins are generated by computer programmes. Their creation – called mining – involves the computer trying to solve an extremely complex mathematical problem. This results in about six Bitcoins being born every hour. Users can see how many Bitcoins there are in existence at any given moment and the currency is designed such that there will never be more than 21 million Bitcoins in circulation.

This limitation to supply is what gives them their value.

All this can seem a bit confusing and even suspicious to newcomers, especially to those who are not technologically minded. And this experimental currency has had some teething problems. Initial excitement over Bitcoins' prospects led to their price expressed in US dollars in 2011 rocketing from $1 to $30 and then collapsing to 30¢. Aside from cases of Bitcoins being stolen in cyberspace, they have yet to command widespread acceptance.

CENTRAL BANKS HERE TO STAY

Despite hostility towards central banks in the wake of the credit crunch, there is no immediate prospect of them disappearing for now. Popular anger has yet to translate into serious calls for their abolition. Fear and uncertainty over what would replace them plays to central banks' advantage for the moment. This gives them room to win back the confidence that they have lost in the early 21st century.

Even if public opinion does eventually turn decisively against central banks – and in favour of their replacement with private money and free banking – the state would not give up its control of money without a struggle. The ability to create money is an enormous power and gives governments much more room for manoeuvre. It would have been almost impossible, for example, for governments to wage two world wars on the scale they did without the facility to print money and manipulate borrowing costs.

Experience confirms that the state guards its monopoly control over money extremely jealously. Were people to desert state-issued paper money in favour of gold, for example, governments would almost inevitably resort to illegalisation and confiscation of that metal, just as Roosevelt did in the US in 1930s, as Hitler did shortly after that, and as Mugabe did in 2007.

Nevertheless, central banks cannot afford to be complacent over the coming years. It may well be that a repeat of the deflationary economic collapse of the 1930s is avoided thanks to aggressive policies like quantitative easing, but the next challenge will be to ensure that money-printing does not trigger persistently high inflation or even hyperinflation. Were hyperinflation to occur, it could well seal the fate of central banking in its current form.

To rebuild their credibility, meanwhile, some self-reform by banks is needed. More transparency in the way that the central banks operate is an obvious way to deflect some of the criticisms against them, even if it means sacrificing one aspect of their effectiveness. Less chumminess with other branches of banking is also a good idea.

Endnotes

[168] Thomson Financial Datastream; and Datastream Total Market Japan series TOTMKJP(PE).

[169] 'The Challenge of Central Banking in a Democratic Society', remarks by Chairman Alan Greenspan At the Annual Dinner and Francis Boyer Lecture of The American Enterprise Institute for Public Policy Research, Washington, D.C. (5 December 1996).

[170] Quoted in Thomas Palley, 'Asset Price Bubbles and the Case for Asset-Based Reserve Requirements', *Challenge* 46:3 (May/June 2003).

[171] 'S&P Case-Shiller Composite-20 City Home Price Index', Bloomberg.

[172] Ben Bernanke in an interview on financial news channel CNBC (1 July 2005).

[173] Bloomberg.

[174] Thomson Financial Datastream.

[175] Cited in Alphaville, *Financial Times* (18 November 2011), **ftalphaville.ft.com/blog/2011/11/18/753971/on-misunderstanding-qe-and-uk-inflation**

[176] Paul de Grauwe, 'Europe needs the ECB to step up to the plate', *Financial Times* (19 October 2011).

[177] Reported by Bloomberg (23 December 2011).

[178] Edward Chancellor, *Devil Take the Hindmost: A History of Financial Speculation* (Macmillan, 1999), pp. 31-2.

[179] Japanese discount rate less Japanese consumer prices, Thomson Financial Datastream.

[180] Thomson Financial Datastream, Japanese Land Price index Residential Areas in 6 big cities, non-seasonally adjusted, JPCITYPRF.

[181] Ryunoshin Kamikawa, 'The Bubble Economy and the Bank of Japan', *Osaka University Law Review* 53 (2006), pp. 105-135.

[182] **blogs.worldbank.org/prospects/do-taylor-rule-deviations-contribute-to-asset-bubbles**

[183] Remarks by Governor Ben S. Bernanke at the Sandridge Lecture, Virginia Association of Economists, Richmond, Virginia (10 March 2005), **www.federalreserve.gov/boarddocs/speeches/2005/200503102/default.htm**

[184] John B. Taylor, 'The Financial Crisis and the Policy Responses: An Empirical Analysis of What Went Wrong', Stanford University (November 2008).

[185] Bloomberg: TINSA Tasaciones Inmobiliarias S.A, Irish House Price Index.

[186] 'Spain: Selected Issues', International Monetary Fund, IMF Country Report No. 09/129 (April 2009).

[187] John Bruton in a speech to the Google Leaders Forum in Dublin (21 July 2011), **www.johnbruton.com**

[188] *Investors Chronicle* data.

[189] **www.usinflationcalculator.com**

[190] Thomson Financial Datastream, Euro area CPI all items, non-seasonally adjusted.

[191] David Blanchflower, 'The Second Great Depression', *New Statesman* (7 July 2011).

[192] Jim Cramer, 'What's the real unemployment rate?', on the Judith Regan show, Sirius FM (13 November 2009).

[193] Joseph B. Treaster, *Paul Volcker: The Making of a Financial Legend* (John Wiley & Sons, 2005).

[194] **www.ronpaul.com/congress/legislation/111th-congress-200910/audit-the-federal-reserve-hr-1207**

[195] Karen K. Lewis, 'Why doesn't society minimise central bank secrecy?', Working Paper No. 3397, National Bureau of Economic Research (July 1990).

[196] Bradley Keoun and Phil Kuntz, 'Wall Street Aristocracy got $1.2 trillion in Secret Loans', Bloomberg (22 August 2011).

[197] 'GAO Finds Serious conflicts at the Fed' (19 October 2011), www.sanders.senate.gov/newsroom/news/?id=BFA0CBEC-CCE1-4520-8899-122C8B719105

[198] Data from Robert Shiller; *Financial Times*; and Foundation for the Study of Cycles.

[199] 'US Business Cycle Expansions and Contractions', National Bureau of Economic Research www.nber.org/cycles/cyclesmain.html

[200] James Wilson, 'Machines with Midas touch swap chocolate for gold bars', *Financial Times* (17 June 2009).

CONCLUSION

FEAR AND GREED have been among the most powerful forces in investment for at least as long as financial markets have existed. But the early 21st century has surely been a period of fear and greed writ large. This is especially true in Western societies, where a combination of terrorism, a vicious credit crunch and the growing power of emerging nations have left citizens feeling less physically secure, more financially precarious, and less self-assured about their standing in the world than they have for decades.

At the same time, the wealth we see displayed around us each day is more conspicuous than ever before. The desire to join the ranks of the rich surely contributed to much of the reckless and short-termist behaviour that culminated in the devastating financial crisis of 2007 onwards, from the creation of aggressive new derivative products to the numerous cases of major fraud that have come to light in rapid succession.

This heightened atmosphere of fear and greed is unlikely to abate in the years ahead. Reasons to be fearful are plentiful, from the potential collapse of the world's second most important currency, to national bankruptcies, to the threats of weak economic growth and financial repression. The spectacle of institutions heavily implicated in the financial crisis now reaping huge gains using cheap money supplied by the authorities could send a dangerous moral message to society about the benefits of greed, meanwhile.

The flipside of the outsized risks that we investors face in the coming years is, of course, outsized opportunities. In order to exploit these opportunities, we need to learn from history. It is the experience of past crises that leads me to believe that the lost era for stocks in the developed world has not yet run its course, and that the terrific bull market in gold has further to go. I also believe that history bears a stark warning about how governments are likely to go about easing their indebtedness, and the likely harm that will be inflicted upon bondholders and bank depositors.

Surely one of the most powerful lessons of the credit crisis to date is that we cannot always rely on receiving protection from our purported protectors. This is certainly true in the case of financial regulators, who have repeatedly proved ineffective just when they were needed most. Likewise, monetary authorities around the world have already been seen to be readier to bolster the banking and political classes, typically at the expense of the ordinary saver.

"Good" investment ideas alone are insufficient. An effective investment strategy may start out with sound investment ideas, but can only be executed if proper financing is in place. The periods when opportunities are most abundant are typically also the times when funding is scarcest. I have occasionally witnessed even large and very sophisticated investors missing out, essentially because of a failure to plan ahead.

Of course, successful investing begins with having a clear view on the world, markets and asset valuations. This is no longer enough nowadays, however. In today's world, the most successful investors must not only be able to assess what other market participants think and expect but also anticipate how these other participants' opinions are likely to evolve in the future. This is no easy task. The reassuring thing for us is that most people think they know exactly what they are doing, and this is when trouble begins for them. In the words of famous investor Howard Marks: "It is frightening to think that you might not know something but more frightening to think that, by and large, the world is run by people who have faith they know exactly what's going on."

Nicolas Sarkis

INDEX

9/11 attacks 50, 128-32, 145-6

A

Acambis (biotechnology firm) 134
accountability (of central banks) 207-8
accounting regulations 163-6
advance-fee frauds 174-5
advertising 30
AIG (American International Group) 207-8
Alfonsín, President Raúl 98
American Scientist (magazine) 139
anthrax scare 132-5
Argentinian default (2001-2002) 97-102
Arthur Andersen (auditing firm) 163
Asian Crisis (1997) 67, 79, 95
Asian Development Bank 139
asymmetric information 175
austerity measures 92, 100-1, 121, 197
austral (Argentinian currency) 97
Austrian school of economics 27, 197-8, 203, 209-10
'availability heuristic' 144
avian influenza 139-42

B

Bair, Sheila 162
Bank of England (BoE) 33, 160, 195, 198, 202, 206
bankers 189-90, 205
Banking Act (1933) 155-6
Bank of Japan (BoJ) 193-5, 199-200, 204
Barings Bank 179-80
Baroin, François 116
Basel III rules 162
Bennett, John G. 176-7, 178
Bernanke, Ben 192-3, 194, 200-1, 205
Bhattacharya, Utpal 183-4
Biota (biotechnology company) 141
bioterrorism 132-5
bird flu (avian influenza) 139-42
Bitcoins (virtual currency) 211-12
Blanchflower, David 204
Blankfein, Lloyd 208
BMO Nesbitt Burns (brokerage house) 139-40
Bolton, Anthony 73
bonds
    and credit crunch 144
    and defaults 100, 103
    and euro crisis 110-11, 117, 122
    and financial repression 36
    historic performance of 1

and lost eras (in equities) 13-14, 17
low yields from 34-5, 38-9
and quantitative easing 33
Booker, Christopher 131-2, 136
boom/bust cycles 28, 197-8, 203-4, 210
borrowing costs 23, 97, 111-2, 115, 117, 120, 153-4, 199
Bramdean Alternatives (asset management firm) 177
BRIC economies 68-70
Bruton, John 201-2
bubbles 5-7, 67-73, 190-2, 197-8
Burd, Professor Andrew 136-7
Business Week (magazine) 17-18
'buy-and-hold' investing 2, 11, 15

C

Cameron, David 157-8, 167n
capital export restrictions 122-3
capital-reserve requirements 88
Carrio, Elisa 99
cash 1, 13-14
Cavallo, Domingo 98-9, 101
'caveat emptor' (buyer beware) 166
central banks
    and bubbles 190-2
    criticism of 189-90, 212
    and deflation 47-8
    future of 204-9, 212-13
    and inflation 202-3
    and interest rates 27, 54, 197-201, 203-4
    and lost eras (in equities) 10
    monetary policy of 197-204
    and quantitative easing 32-3, 194-6
    response to events 193-6
central planning 73
Chancellor, Edward 6, 198
cheap credit 27, 71-2, 98, 197-8
Chernomyrdin, Prime Minister Viktor 94
Chiesi, Danielle 185
CMAT (Chuo Mitsui Asset Trust) 158-9
competitiveness 113-14
consumerism 30, 41

contagion, spread of 115-17
Cooper, Sherry 140
copper prices 17
corporate governance 78
corruption 80, 93
CPI (Consumer Price Index) 37-8, 43-5
Cramer, Jim 205
credit card debt 30
credit crunch, 43, 74, 114, 142-4, 194-5, 201, 217-18
credit ratings 90, 115, 116, 125n
creditworthiness 94-5
crime 187
'cult of equity' 1-2, 18
currencies
    devaluation of 95-7, 99, 101, 103
    and gold 52-3, 209-11
    returning to sovereign 120-1, 123-4
    vulnerability of 107-8

D

Davis Polk (law firm) 156
debt clocks 22
deception 37-8
defaults
    causes of 87-91, 93-6, 97-9
    and euro crisis 120
    impact of 87, 91, 96, 100-2
    lessons learned from 102-3
    response to 91-2, 96-7
deflation 14, 32-3, 46-8, 193-5, 204, 210
deleveraging
    and economic growth 24, 32, 34
    effects of 21, 29-31
    and financial repression 35-8
    and inflation 33-5, 39
    and investment strategy 38-9
Department of Justice (DoJ) 151
Der Spiegel (magazine) 181-2
devaluation 91, 92, 95-7, 99, 101, 103
direct ownership (in gold) 57-8
dividends 11, 16-17, 52, 58-9, 68
Dixon, Dr Patrick 137

Dodd-Franks Act (2010) 155-6, 160, 161
Draghi, Mario 111-12
due diligence 175, 178

E

earnings yield 82
ECB (European Central Bank)
    and commercial bank lending 36
    criticism of 196-7
    and euro crisis 109, 110-12, 123-4
    monetary policy of 200-2, 204
economic growth
    and bond yields 34-5
    and deflation 210
    and deleveraging 24, 34
    and euro crisis 112
    and indebtedness 23-4, 31-2
    and returns 65-6
economic reforms 88-9, 98
economic risk 74-7
Economist, The (magazine) 79
Edwards, Albert 72-3
EFSF (European Financial Stability Facility) 115-16
email scams 174-5
emerging markets
    access to 11-12
    bubbles in 67-73
    growth of 63-4, 217
    and indebtedness 23
    investment strategies 64-6, 81-4
    and lost eras (in equities) 11-13
    and risk 74-80
Enron (energy trading firm) 135, 163-4
Equitable Life (insurance company) 149-50, 152-3
equities
    and central banks 190-1
    'cult of' 1-2, 18
    and deleveraging 39
    effects of fear on 127-8, 131-2, 134-5, 137-8, 141-6
    and euro crisis 112, 123-4
    and gold 51-2, 60
    historic performance of 1-2

    and inflation 76
    lost eras in see lost eras
    overvaluation of 7-9, 15-17
    and takeover bids 186
    see also emerging markets
European Stability Mechanism (ESM) 115-17, 120
euro (currency)
    creation of 109
    and government borrowing 110
    international support for 117-18
    potential collapse of 107-8, 117, 120
    and quantitative easing 110-11, 112, 124
    and return to sovereign currencies 120-1, 123-4
euro bonds 110
Eurostat (accounting regulator) 165
exchange rates 89-90, 92, 95
exchange-traded funds (ETFs) 12, 52, 53, 55-6
exclusivity 178
exports 67, 73, 92, 94-5, 101-2, 119, 124

F

Federal Bureau of Investigation (FBI) 133
fear 127-32, 134-5, 137-8, 141-6, 217
Federal Deposit Insurance Corporation 162
Federal Reserve
    and bubbles 190-2
    and deflation 47-8
    and interest rates 54, 90
    and lost eras (in equities) 10, 16-17
    monetary policy of 200-1, 205-8
    and quantitative easing 33, 194-5
    and restrictions on gold ownership 57
Fekter, Maria 116
Ferguson, James 195
financial freedom 36-7
financial modelling 152, 154, 178
financial repression 35-8

Financial Services Authority (FSA)
156-7
financial statements 80
Fisher, Professor Irving 6, 17, 27, 32
Forbes (magazine) 163, 164
Fortune (magazine) 163
Foundation for New Era Philanthropy
175-7
fraudsters 170-9
Freedman, Samuel G. 172
Friedman, Professor Milton 202
front-running 151

G

Gaidar, Yegor 93-4
Galleon Group (hedge fund) 184-5
Gil-Diaz, Francisco 89
Glass-Steagall Act (1933) 155-6
Global Crossing (telecommunications
company) 135
globalisation 82
Goel, Rajiv 185
gold
    as backing for currency 209-11
    comparison with other assets 51-3,
    60
    and deflation 46-8
    and deleveraging 39
    future performance of 42-3, 53-5
    and inflation 43-8, 54
    investing in 55-60
    and lost eras (in equities) 14-15
    performance during instability 49-
    50
    price-fixing of 46-7, 59
    rising price of 41-2, 53, 54-5
Goldman Sachs (investment bank) 165,
208
gold-mining stocks 58-60
Government Accountability Office
(US) 208
Grauwe, Paul de 196
Great Depression (US)
    and central banks 194
    and deflationary collapse 32
    and gold 46-7, 209

as lost era (in equities) 12, 14
    modern comparisons 29-30, 140,
    142-3
    psychological effects of 29-31
Greenfield, Robert 211
Greenspan, Alan 190-3, 200
growth stocks (in emerging markets) 84
guaranteed annuities 150
Gutiérrez, Gustavo 99

H

Halley, Edmund 149
Hannan, Daniel 206
Hartzell, Oscar 175, 178, 187
hedge funds 159-60
high-yield corporate bonds 122
Hitler, Adolf 213
Horlick, Nicola 177
household debt 25-6
house prices 201-2
hyperinflation 46, 76, 98, 109, 203, 213
hyper-vigilance 129, 130

I

IBM (technology group) 185
Impex (oil developer) 158
imports 90, 98-9, 101
income tax 159
indebtedness
    and boom/bust cycles 28
    causes of 25-7
    and economic growth 23-4, 31-2
    and emerging markets 74-6
    and financial repression 35
    and leverage 22-3
    psychological effects of 29-31
    reducing 31-5
    see also defaults
industrial value added (IVA) growth 79
inflation
    and central banks 202-3
    and debt reduction 31-2, 33-5
    and defaults 94, 97-8

and emerging markets 75-7
and euro crisis 111, 125n
and financial repression 36, 37-8
and gold 43-8, 54, 209-10
and interest rates 34-5, 45, 54-5
and lost eras (in equities) 9-10, 13-14, 17
and quantitative easing 43, 195-6, 213
insider trading 80, 158-9, 183-6
Intel (microchip manufacturer) 185
International Monetary Fund (IMF)
and defaults 91-2, 96, 98, 100
and euro crisis 113-14, 117-18, 121
interest rates
and central banks 27, 54, 197-201, 203-4, 206
and credit crunch 143
and defaults 90
and inflation 34-5, 45, 54-5
and LIBOR market 153-4
International Accounting Standards Board (IASB) 76

K

Kamikawa, Ryunoshin 199-200
Kennedy, Joseph 18
Keqiang, Li 79
Kerviel, Jérôme 181-2
Kindleberger, Charles 68
Kumar, Anil 184-5

L

labour costs 113
Lay, Kenneth 163
Lee Kuan Yew 160
Leeson, Nick 179-80
Lehman Brothers (financial services firm) 143
Levitt, Arthur 179
life insurance 149
London Inter-bank Offered Rate (LIBOR) market 153-4

lost era (in equities)
continuation of 218
coping with 11-15
defining 2-4
end of 15-18
reasons for 5-10

M

Madoff, Bernie 151-2, 154, 164, 166n, 171-3, 177-9
Madoff, Peter 179
malfeasance risk 78
mal-investment 27, 198
managed exchange-rates 89
management of debt crises 30-1
market valuations 82-3
Markopolous, Harry 152, 154, 178
Marks, Howard 218
mark-to-market accounting 164
Marshall, Cassandra D. 183-4
McKinnon, Professor Ronald 35
McKinsey (management consultancy) 184
McLean, Bethany 164
media 130, 132-5, 136-8, 140-1, 143
Menem, President Carlos 98-9
'merchant model' accounting 164
Merkel, Angela 116, 120
Mexican Peso Crisis (1994) 88-92
Minsky, Hyman 28
'Minsky moment' 28
minutes, release of 207
Mirvis, Tova 173
Moffat, Robert 185-6
monetary policy 197-204
Mugabe, Robert 213
mutual funds 6-7, 144

N

Napier, Russell 17
New York Times (newspaper) 172, 179
Nixon, President Richard 47
North American Free Trade Agreement (NAFTA) (1995) 88

North, Dr Richard 131-2, 136
Noyer, Christian 181

O

online bullion-exchanges 57
Organisation for Economic
  Cooperation and Development
  (OECD)
116
Osterholm, Michael 140
OTC (over-the-counter) markets 161
overvaluation 7-9, 15-17

P

Paris Club 94-5, 102
Paul, Ron 207
Paulson & Co. (hedge fund) 108
Paulson, John 108, 122
pension funds 36-7, 74-5
personal debt 25-6
Personal Investment Authority 150
pharmaceutical stocks 134-5, 141-2
philanthropy 171-3, 175-7
political culture 92-3
Ponzi schemes 151-2, 154, 169, 171-3,
  175-9
post-traumatic stress disorder (PTSD)
  129, 130
Pou, Pedro 99
precautionary credit line (PCL) 118
Prechter, Robert J. 28
Pressman, Professor Steven 175-6
price-to-earnings (PE) ratio 3, 7-8, 16,
  69-70, 76, 82-3
price/volume data 186
PricewaterhouseCoopers (accountancy
  firm) 113
private sector debt 26-7
production costs 113
property rights 57, 78
psychological effects of indebtedness
  29-31
public mood 17-18, 28

Pulmuone Co. (health food company)
  141-2
Putin, President Vladimir 96

Q

quantitative easing (QE)
  and central banks 194-6, 205
  criticism of 194-6
  and debt reduction 32-3
  and defaults 103-4
  and emerging markets 76-7
  and euro crisis 110-11, 112, 124
  and inflation 43, 195-6, 213

R

Rajaratnam, Raj 184-5
Randgold Resources (gold-mining
  firm) 59-60
Randt, Clark T. 79
'rat-trading' 80
regulation
  accounting regulations 163-6
  avoiding 159-61
  consequences of 162
  enforcement of 158-9
  forms of 155-8
regulators 149-55
Retail Price Index (RPI) 33, 195
returns 11-12, 64-6
rigging statistics 37-8, 79
risk 64-5, 74-80, 145-6
Ritter, Professor Jay 65-6, 82
Roach, Stephen 137-8
Roche (pharmaceuticals company) 141
rogue traders 179-83
Roosevelt, President Franklin D. 57,
  213
Rothschild, Baron 145
rule of law 78
Russian default (1998) 92-7

S

Salinas, President Carlos 88-9
Sanders, Bernie 208
Sardelis, Christoforos 165
Sarkozy, President Nicolas 109, 167n
savings 200-1
Schäuble, Wolfgang 116, 120
secrecy 179, 207
Securities and Exchange Commission
    (SEC) 151-2, 154, 164, 178-9
Securities Industries and Financial
    Markets Association (SIFMA)
    178-9
self-justification 171-3
Severe Acute Respiratory Syndrome
    (SARS) 136-8
Shaw, Professor Edward 35
Shiller, Professor Robert 7-8, 192
Shirakawa, Masaaki 193-4
short-selling 123
Sidaoui, José Julián 89-90
Siegel, Professor Jeremy 1-2
'silent generation' 29
Skilling, Jeffrey 164
Slater, Jim 49
Smaghi, Lorenzo Bini 196-7
social and political risk 77-8
social mood 28
social status 170-3
Société Générale (SG) 181-2
'soft budgeting' 93
sovereign currencies, return to 120-1,
    123-4
Spanish flu 138, 139, 146
Spencer, Baldwin 170
St Jude's (children's cancer charity) 171
Stanford, Allen 169-71, 173
Stocks for the Long Run (book) 2
supra-national regulation 157
swap agreements 55-6, 153, 165

T

takeover bids 186
Tamiflu (antiviral drug) 141

taxation 93-4, 159-60
Taylor, John B. 201
Taylor Rule 200-1
technology stocks 5-7, 68-9, 190-1
'tequila crisis 88-92
terrorism 128-30, 132-5, 217
tesobonos (Mexican government
    securities) 89-90
Thomson-Reuters (news agency) 153
'tiger' economies 67, 73
Time (magazine) 29
trade barriers 12
transparency (of central banks) 207
Treasury Bills 45
Trichet, Jean-Claude 111
trust 178-9
Tso, Ivy 129

U

Undertakings for Collective Investment
    in Transferable
    Securities (UCITS) 157
unemployment 29-30, 97-8, 100, 112,
    195-6, 200
unreliable economic data 78-9

V

value stocks (in emerging markets) 84
Volcker, Paul 167n, 205-6
Volcker rule 155-6, 162, 167n

W

wage reduction 113
Wall Street Crash (1929) 3-4, 6, 18
Wall Street Journal Europe (newspaper)
    134
warfare 8-9, 13, 25, 212
War on Terror 9, 25, 37, 129-30
Washington Post (newspaper) 133
Webster, Professor Robert G. 139
welfare provision 29-30, 74-5

Wolff, Guntram 119
World Gold Council 43

Y

Yeager, Leland 211
Yeltsin, Boris 94

Z

Zedillo, President Ernesto 91, 92